THE HOLOCAUST, NEVER TO BE FORGOTTEN:

REFLECTIONS ON THE HOLY SEE'S DOCUMENT
WE REMEMBER

Studies in Judaism and Christianity

Exploration of Issues in the Contemporary Dialogue Between Christians and Jews

Editor in Chief for
Stimulus Books
Helga Croner

Editors
Lawrence Boadt, C.S.P.
Helga Croner
Rabbi Leon Klenicki
Kevin A. Lynch, C.S.P.
Dennis McManus

A STIMULUS BOOK

THE HOLOCAUST, NEVER TO BE FORGOTTEN:

Reflections on the Holy See's Document *We Remember*

Commentaries by
Avery Dulles, S.J. and **Rabbi Leon Klenicki**

with an Address by
Edward Idris Cardinal Cassidy

JUN 2001

A STIMULUS BOOK

PAULIST PRESS ◆ NEW YORK ◆ MAHWAH, N.J.

Acknowledgments

The text of *We Remember: A Reflection on the* Shoah by the Vatican Commission for Religious Relations With the Jews was taken from *Origins,* Vol. 27, pp. 669ff. (the edition dated March 26, 1998). The text of the Address to the American Jewish Committee by Edward Idris Cardinal Cassidy was taken from *Origins,* Vol. 28, pp. 28ff. (the edition dated May 28, 1998).

Cover design by Lynn Else

Library of Congress Cataloging-in-Publication Data

Dulles, Avery Robert, 1918–
    The Holocaust, never to be forgotten : reflections on the Holy See's document "We remember" / commentaries by Avery Dulles and Leon Klenicki; with an address by Cardinal Cassidy to the American Jewish Committee.
        p. cm. — (Stimulus book) (Studies in Judaism and Christianity)
    "We remember : a reflection on the *Shoah*" / Commission for Religious Relations with the Jews.
    Includes bibliographical references.
    ISBN 0-8091-3985-5 (alk. paper)
    1. Holocaust, Jewish (1939–1945)—Influence. 2. Catholic Church—Relations—Judaism. 3. Judaism—Relations—Catholic Church. I. Klenicki, Leon. II. Cassidy, Edward Idris. III. Catholic Church. Commission for Religious Relations with the Jews. We remember. IV. Title. V. Series. VI. Series: Studies in Judaism and Christianity.

D804.3.D83 2001
940.53′18—dc21

                                                                00-069299

Published by Paulist Press
997 Macarthur Boulevard
Mahwah, New Jersey 07430

www.paulistpress.com

Printed and bound in the
United States of America

Contents

Introduction by Lawrence Boadt, C.S.P.

Important milestones in the development of human understanding are rarely achieved without generating even more issues and further questions than had originally been considered. One thinks, for example, of the proclamation of the *Magna Carta,* which the English barons forced on King John I in 1215, or the impact of the Vatican II documents on interfaith relations. Although hailed as vital turning points for society both by contemporary observers and by future generations of historians, such significant events not only highlight new directions and opportunities for the communities involved, but also many of the shortcomings and missing elements that still need to be addressed if they are to become a mutually accepted vision for all parties to the discussion.

It is in this vein that we might best view the official publication of the document of the Vatican's Commission for Religious Relations with the Jews that was issued on March 6, 1998, and titled, *We Remember: A Reflection on the* Shoah. It is clearly an important statement for the Roman Catholic Church, directed first of all to its own members, that puts the church itself on record acknowledging not only the tragic historical reality of the Holocaust

(*Shoah*) but also responsibility for the Christian anti-Semitic attitudes that contributed to its happening. Moreover, the statement adds a clear declaration of repentance and a rejection of all anti-Semitism among church members and in church teaching. But it was also an important document for the Jewish community as well. It was prepared in response to Jewish requests for a firm acknowledgment of the terrible involvement of Christian individuals and Christian teachings of contempt that made the *Shoah* possible, and for a definite act of repentance (*teshuva*) that would further the vital act of healing this great evil.

Once issued, *We Remember* has received wide praise, some disappointment, and much controversy. Because it does have broad implications for the ongoing relationship of Jews and Catholics (and all Christians), we should expect and welcome critical evaluations and pointed questions to arise both from what it says and what it does not say. It will never become the important catalyst for healing and for growth in mutual respect and dialogue until such reflections have been heard, addressed, and have advanced our conversation beyond the document itself.

This small volume brings together the statement itself, Cardinal Edward Idris Cassidy's reflection on its history and the controversy surrounding its appearance, and two reflections by highly respected theologians in the Catholic-Jewish dialogue. Jesuit theologian Avery Dulles has written prolifically on the foundations of Christian faith; Rabbi Leon Klenicki has been equally productive on the fundamental principles that must govern Jewish-Christian interfaith relations. Both have committed much of their theological careers to exploring the meaning of God's revelation in the Jewish and Christian traditions, and both consistently have been sensitive to the deepest beliefs of the other's faith community. Hopefully, the insights and suggestions that they offer in this volume will invite many more Christians and Jews to speak together with the same frankness and respect, and address the meaning of the *Shoah* honestly and in a spirit of building bridges to further understanding. Above all, may it summon all who read the thoughtful wisdom of these two people of faith to a step forward in the dialogue: for Christians, a call to the commitment to concrete acts of healing for the sin of anti-Semitism through two thousand years; and for Jews, an invitation to heal the trust between victim and oppressor by an offer of forgiveness to those who are truly repentant for the terrible evil they have either caused or participated in, and have converted in heart and in deed for the future.

LAWRENCE BOADT, C.S.P.
Publisher of the Paulist Press

WE REMEMBER:
A REFLECTION ON
THE *SHOAH*

The Document of the Holy See

Commission for Religious Relations with the Jews

To my Venerable Brother
Cardinal Edward Idris Cassidy

On numerous occasions during my Pontificate I have recalled with a sense of deep sorrow the sufferings of the Jewish people during the Second World War. The crime which has become known as the *Shoah* remains an indelible stain on the history of the century that is coming to a close.

As we prepare for the beginning of the Third Millennium of Christianity, the Church is aware that the joy of a Jubilee is above all the joy that is based on the forgiveness of sins and reconciliation with God and neighbour. Therefore she encourages her sons and daughters to purify their hearts, through repentance of past errors and infidelities. She calls them to place themselves humbly before the Lord and examine themselves on the responsibility which they too have for the evils of our time.

It is my fervent hope that the document: *We Remember: A Reflection on the* Shoah, which the Commission for Religious Relations with the Jews has prepared under your direction, will indeed help to heal the wounds of past misunderstandings and injustices. May it enable memory to play its necessary part in the process of shaping a future in which the unspeakable iniquity of the *Shoah* will never again be possible. May the Lord of history guide the efforts of Catholics and Jews and all men and women of good will as they work together for a world of true respect for the life and dignity of every human being, for all have been created in the image and likeness of god.

JOHN PAUL II
From the Vatican, 12 March 1998

We Remember:
A Reflection on the *Shoah*

Commission for Religious Relations with the Jews

I. The tragedy of the *Shoah* and the duty of remembrance

The 20th century is fast coming to a close and a new Millennium of the Christian era is about to dawn. The 2000th anniversary of the Birth of Jesus Christ calls all Christians, and indeed invites all men and women, to seek to discern in the passage of history the signs of divine Providence at work, as well as the ways in which the image of the Creator in man has been offended and disfigured.

This reflection concerns one of the main areas in which Catholics can seriously take to heart the summons which Pope John Paul II has addressed to them in his Apostolic Letter *Tertio Millennio Adveniente:* "It is appropriate that, as the Second Millennium of Christianity draws to a close, the Church should become more fully conscious of the sinfulness of her children, recalling all those times in history when they departed from the spirit of Christ and his Gospel and, instead of offering to the world the witness of a life inspired by the values of faith, indulged in ways of thinking and acting which were truly forms of counter-witness and scandal".[1]

This century has witnessed an unspeakable tragedy, which can never be forgotten: the attempt by the Nazi regime to exterminate the Jewish people, with the consequent killing of millions of Jews. Women and men, old and young, children and infants, for the sole reason of their Jewish origin, were persecuted and deported. Some were killed immediately, while others were degraded, illtreated, tortured and utterly robbed of their human dignity, and then murdered. Very few of those who entered the Camps survived, and those who did remained scarred for life. This was the *Shoah*. It is a major fact of the history of this century, a fact which still concerns us today.

Before this horrible genocide, which the leaders of nations and Jewish communities themselves found hard to believe at the very moment when it was being mercilessly put into effect, no one can remain indifferent, least of all the Church, by reason of her very close bonds of spiritual kinship with the Jewish people and her remembrance of the injustices of the past. The Church's relationship to the Jewish people is unlike the one she shares with any other religion.[2] However, it is not only a question of recalling the past. The common future of Jews and Christians demands that we remember, for "there is no future without memory".[3] History itself is *memoria futuri*.

---

[1] Pope John Paul II, Apostolic Letter *Tertio Millennio Adveniente,* 10 November 1994, 33: *AAS* 87 (1995), 25.

[2] Cf. Pope John Paul II. *Speech at the Synagogue of Rome,* 13 April 1986, 4: *AAS* 78 (1986), 1120.

[3] Pope John Paul II, *Angelus Prayer,* 11 June 1995: *Insegnamenti* 18/1, 1995, 1712.

In addressing this reflection to our brothers and sisters of the Catholic Church throughout the world, we ask all Christians to join us in meditating on the catastrophe which befell the Jewish people, and on the moral imperative to ensure that never again will selfishness and hatred grow to the point of sowing such suffering and death.[4] Most especially, we ask our Jewish friends, "whose terrible fate has become a symbol of the aberrations of which man is capable when he turns against God",[5] to hear us with open hearts.

II. What we must remember

While bearing their unique witness to the Holy One of Israel and to the *Torah,* the Jewish people have suffered much at different times and in many places. But the *Shoah* was certainly the worst suffering of all. The inhumanity with which the Jews were persecuted and massacred during this century is beyond the capacity of words to convey. All this was done to them for the sole reason that they were Jews.

The very magnitude of the crime raises many questions. Historians, sociologists, political philosophers, psychologists and theologians are all trying to learn more about the reality of the *Shoah* and its causes. Much scholarly study still remains to be done. But such an event cannot be fully measured by the ordinary criteria of historical research alone. It calls for a "moral and religious memory"

---

[4] Cf. Pope John Paul II, *Address to Jewish Leaders in Budapest,* 18 August 1991, 4: *Insegnamenti* 14/2, 1991, 349.

[5] Pope John Paul II, Encyclical Letter *Centesimus Annus,* 1 May 1991, 17: *AAS* 83 (1991), 814–815.

and, particularly among Christians, a very serious reflection on what gave rise to it.

The fact that the *Shoah* took place in Europe, that is, in countries of long-standing Christian civilization, raises the question of the relation between the Nazi persecution and the attitudes down the centuries of Christians towards the Jews.

III. Relations between Jews and Christians

The history of relations between Jews and Christians is a tormented one. His Holiness Pope John Paul II has recognized this fact in his repeated appeals to Catholics to see where we stand with regard to our relations with the Jewish people.[6] In effect, the balance of these relations over two thousand years has been quite negative.[7]

At the dawn of Christianity, after the crucifixion of Jesus, there arose disputes between the early Church and the Jewish leaders and people who, in their devotion to the Law, on occasion violently opposed the preachers of the Gospel and the first Christians. In the pagan Roman Empire, Jews were legally protected by the privileges granted by the Emperor and the authorities at first made no distinction between Jewish and Christian communities. Soon however, Christians incurred the persecution of the State. Later, when the Emperors themselves converted to Christianity, they at first continued to guarantee Jewish privileges. But Christian

---

[6] Cf. Pope John Paul II, *Address to Delegates of Episcopal Conferences for Catholic-Jewish Relations,* 6 March 1982: *Insegnamenti,* 5/1, 1982, 743–747.

[7] Cf. Holy See's Commission for Religious Relations with the Jews, *Notes on the correct way to present the Jews and Judaism in preaching and catechesis in the Roman Catholic Church,* 24 June 1985, VI, 1: *Ench. Vat.* 9, 1656.

mobs who attacked pagan temples sometimes did the same to synagogues, not without being influenced by certain interpretations of the New Testament regarding the Jewish people as a whole. "In the Christian world–I do not say on the part of the Church as such–erroneous and unjust interpretations of the New Testament regarding the Jewish people and their alleged culpability have circulated for too long, engendering feelings of hostility towards this people".[8] Such interpretations of the New Testament have been totally and definitively rejected by the Second Vatican Council.[9]

Despite the Christian preaching of love for all, even for one's enemies, the prevailing mentality down the centuries penalized minorities and those who were in any way "different". Sentiments of anti-Judaism in some Christian quarters, and the gap which existed between the Church and the Jewish people, led to a generalized discrimination, which ended at times in expulsions or attempts at forced conversions. In a large part of the "Christian" world, until the end of the 18th century, those who were not Christian did not always enjoy a fully guaranteed juridical status. Despite that fact, Jews throughout Christendom held on to their religious traditions and communal customs. They were therefore looked upon with a certain suspicion and mistrust. In times of crisis such as famine, war, pestilence or social tensions, the Jewish minority was sometimes taken as a scapegoat and became the victim of violence, looting, even massacres.

By the end of the 18th century and the beginning of the 19th century, Jews generally had achieved an equal standing

---

[8] Cf. Pope John Paul II, *Speech to Symposium on the roots of anti-Judaism,* 31 October 1997, 1: *L'Osservatore Romano,* 1 November 1997, p. 6.

[9] Cf. Second Vatican Ecumenical Council, *Nostra Aetate,* 4.

with other citizens in most States and a certain number of them held influential positions in society. But in that same historical context, notably in the 19th century, a false and exacerbated nationalism took hold. In a climate of eventful social change, Jews were often accused of exercising an influence disproportionate to their numbers. Thus there began to spread in varying degrees throughout most of Europe an anti-Judaism that was essentially more sociological and political than religious.

At the same time, theories began to appear which denied the unity of the human race, affirming an original diversity of races. In the 20th century, National Socialism in Germany used these ideas as a pseudo-scientific basis for a distinction between so called Nordic-Aryan races and supposedly inferior races. Furthermore, an extremist form of nationalism was heightened in Germany by the defeat of 1918 and the demanding conditions imposed by the victors, with the consequence that many saw in National Socialism a solution to their country's problems and cooperated politically with this movement.

The Church in Germany replied by condemning racism. The condemnation first appeared in the preaching of some of the clergy, in the public teaching of the Catholic Bishops, and in the writings of lay Catholic journalists. Already in February and March 1931, Cardinal Bertram of Breslau, Cardinal Faulhaber and the Bishops of Bavaria, the Bishops of the Province of Cologne and those of the Province of Freiburg published pastoral letters condemning National Socialism, with its idolatry of race and of the State.[10] The well-known Advent sermons of Cardinal Faulhaber in 1933,

---

[10] Cf. B. Statiewski (Ed.), *Akten deutscher Bischöfe über die Lage der Kirche,* 1933–1945, vol. I, 1933–1934 (Mainz 1968), Appendix.

the very year in which National Socialism came to power, at which not just Catholics but also Protestants and Jews were present, clearly expressed rejection of the Nazi anti-semitic propaganda.[11] In the wake of the *Kristallnacht,* Bernhard Lichtenberg, Provost of Berlin Cathedral, offered public prayers for the Jews. He was later to die at Dachau and has been declared Blessed.

Pope Pius XI too condemned Nazi racism in a solemn way in his Encyclical Letter *Mit brennender Sorge,*[12] which was read in German churches on Passion Sunday 1937, a step which resulted in attacks and sanctions against members of the clergy. Addressing a group of Belgian pilgrims on 6 September 1938, Pius XI asserted: "Anti-Semitism is unacceptable. Spiritually, we are all Semites".[13] Pius XII, in his very first Encyclical, *Summi Pontificatus,*[14] of 20 October 1939, warned against theories which denied the unity of the human race and against the deification of the State, all of which he saw as leading to a real "hour of darkness".[15]

IV. Nazi anti-Semitism and the *Shoah*

Thus we cannot ignore the difference which exists between **anti-Semitism,** based on theories contrary to the constant teaching of the Church on the unity of the human race and on the equal dignity of all races and peoples, and the long-standing sentiments of mistrust and hostility that

---

[11] Cf. L. Volk, *Der Bayerische Episkopat und der Nationalsozialismus 1930–1934* (Mainz 1966), pp. 170–174.

[12] The Encyclical is dated 14 March 1937: *AAS* 29 (1937), 145–167.

[13] *La Documentation Catholique,* 29 (1938), col. 1460.

[14] *AAS* 31 (1939), 413–453.

[15] *Ibid.,* 449.

we call **anti-Judaism,** of which, unfortunately, Christians also have been guilty.

The National Socialist ideology went even further, in the sense that it refused to acknowledge any transcendent reality as the source of life and the criterion of moral good. Consequently, a human group, and the State with which it was identified, arrogated to itself an absolute status and determined to remove the very existence of the Jewish people, a people called to witness to the one God and the Law of the Covenant. At the level of theological reflection we cannot ignore the fact that not a few in the Nazi party not only showed aversion to the idea of divine Providence at work in human affairs, but gave proof of a definite hatred directed at God himself. Logically, such an attitude also led to a rejection of Christianity, and a desire to see the Church destroyed or at least subjected to the interests of the Nazi State.

It was this extreme ideology which became the basis of the measures taken, first to drive the Jews from their homes and then to exterminate them. The *Shoah* was the work of a thoroughly modern neo-pagan regime. Its anti-Semitism had its roots outside of Christianity and, in pursuing its aims, it did not hesitate to oppose the Church and persecute her members also.

But it may be asked whether the Nazi persecution of the Jews was not made easier by the anti-Jewish prejudices imbedded in some Christian minds and hearts. Did anti-Jewish sentiment among Christians make them less sensitive, or even indifferent, to the persecutions launched against the Jews by National Socialism when it reached power?

Any response to this question must take into account that we are dealing with the history of people's attitudes and ways of thinking, subject to multiple influences. Moreover,

many people were altogether unaware of the "final solution" that was being put into effect against a whole people;
others were afraid for themselves and those near to them;
some took advantage of the situation; and still others were
moved by envy. A response would need to be given case by
case. To do this, however, it is necessary to know what precisely motivated people in a particular situation.

At first the leaders of the Third Reich sought to expel
the Jews. Unfortunately, the governments of some Western
countries of Christian tradition, including some in North
and South America, were more than hesitant to open their
borders to the persecuted Jews. Although they could not
foresee how far the Nazi hierarchs would go in their crimi-
nal intentions, the leaders of those nations were aware of the
hardships and dangers to which Jews living in the territories
of the Third Reich were exposed. The closing of borders to
Jewish emigration in those circumstances, whether due to
anti-Jewish hostility or suspicion, political cowardice or
shortsightedness, or national selfishness, lays a heavy burden of conscience on the authorities in question.

In the lands where the Nazis undertook mass deportations, the brutality which surrounded these forced movements of helpless people should have led to suspect the
worst. Did Christians give every possible assistance to
those being persecuted, and in particular to the persecuted
Jews?

Many did, but others did not. Those who did help to
save Jewish lives as much as was in their power, even to the
point of placing their own lives in danger, must not be forgotten. During and after the war, Jewish communities and
Jewish leaders expressed their thanks for all that had been
done for them, including what Pope Pius XII did personally

or through his representatives to save hundreds of thousands of Jewish lives.[16] Many Catholic bishops, priests, religious and laity have been honoured for this reason by the State of Israel.

Nevertheless, as Pope John Paul II has recognized, alongside such courageous men and women, the spiritual resistance and concrete action of other Christians was not that which might have been expected from Christ's followers. We cannot know how many Christians in countries occupied or ruled by the Nazi powers or their allies were horrified at the disappearance of their Jewish neighbours and yet were not strong enough to raise their voices in protest. For Christians, this heavy burden of conscience of

---

[16] The wisdom of Pope Pius XII's diplomacy was publicly acknowledged on a number of occasions by representative Jewish Organizations and personalities. For example, on 7 September 1945, Dr. Joseph Nathan, who represented the Italian Hebrew Commission, stated: "Above all, we acknowledge the Supreme Pontiff and the religious men and women who, executing the directives of the Holy Father, recognized the persecuted as their brothers and, with effort and abnegation, hastened to help us, disregarding the terrible dangers to which they were exposed" (*L'Osservatore Romano,* 8 September 1945, p. 2). On 21 September of that same year, Pius XII received in audience Dr. A. Leo Kubowitzki, Secretary General of the World Jewish Congress, who came to present "to the Holy Father, in the name of the Union of Israelitic Communities, warmest thanks for the efforts of the Catholic Church on behalf of Jews throughout Europe during the War" (*L'Osservatore Romano,* 23 September 1945, p. 1). On Thursday, 29 November 1945, the Pope met about 80 representatives of Jewish refugees from various concentration camps in Germany, who expressed "their great honour at being able to thank the Holy Father personally for his generosity towards those persecuted during the Nazi-Fascist period" (*L'Osservatore Romano,* 30 November 1945, p. 1). In 1958, at the death of Pope Pius XII, Golda Meir sent an eloquent message: "We share in the grief of humanity. When fearful martyrdom came to our people, the voice of the Pope was raised for its victims. The life of our times was enriched by a voice speaking out about great moral truths above the tumult of daily conflict. We mourn a great servant of peace".

their brothers and sisters during the Second World War must be a call to penitence.[17]

We deeply regret the errors and failures of those sons and daughters of the Church. We make our own what is said in the Second Vatican Council's Declaration *Nostra Aetate,* which unequivocally affirms: "The Church...mindful of her common patrimony with the Jews, and motivated by the Gospel's spiritual love and by no political considerations, deplores the hatred, persecutions and displays of anti-Semitism directed against the Jews at any time and from any source".[18]

We recall and abide by what Pope John Paul II, addressing the leaders of the Jewish community in Strasbourg in 1988, stated: "I repeat again with you the strongest condemnation of anti-Semitism and racism, which are opposed to the principles of Christianity."[19] The Catholic Church therefore repudiates every persecution against a people or human group anywhere, at any time. She absolutely condemns all forms of genocide, as well as the racist ideologies which give rise to them. Looking back over this century, we are deeply saddened by the violence that has enveloped whole groups of peoples and nations. We recall in particular the massacre of the Armenians, the countless victims in Ukraine in the 1930s, the genocide of the Gypsies, which was also the result of racist ideas, and similar tragedies which have occurred in America, Africa and the Balkans. Nor do we forget the millions of victims of

---

[17] Cf. Pope John Paul II, *Address to the New Ambassador of the Federal Republic of Germany in the Holy See,* 8 November 1990, 2: *AAS* 83 (1991), 587–588.

[18] *Loc. cit.,* no. 4.

[19] Address to Jewish Leaders, Strasbourg, 9 October 1988, no. 8: *Insegnamenti* 11/3, 1988, 1134.

totalitarian ideology in the Soviet Union, in China, Cambodia and elsewhere. Nor can we forget the drama of the Middle East, the elements of which are well known. Even as we make this reflection, "many human beings are still their brothers' victims".[20]

V. Looking together to a common future

Looking to the future of relations between Jews and Christians, in the first place we appeal to our Catholic brothers and sisters to renew the awareness of the Hebrew roots of their faith. We ask them to keep in mind that Jesus was a descendant of David; that the Virgin Mary and the Apostles belonged to the Jewish people; that the Church draws sustenance from the root of that good olive tree on to which have been grafted the wild olive branches of the Gentiles (cf. *Rom* 11:17–24); that the Jews are our dearly beloved brothers, indeed in a certain sense they are "our elder brothers".[21]

At the end of this Millennium the Catholic Church desires to express her deep sorrow for the failures of her sons and daughters in every age. This is an act of repentance (*teshuva*), since, as members of the Church, we are linked to the sins as well as the merits of all her children. The Church approaches with deep respect and great compassion the experience of extermination, the *Shoah*, suffered by the Jewish people during World War II. It is not a matter of mere words, but indeed of binding commitment. "We would risk causing

---

[20] Pope John Paul II, *Address to the Diplomatic Corps,* 15 January 1994, 9: *AAS* 86 (1994), 816.

[21] Pope John Paul II, *Speech at the Synagogue of Rome,* 13 April 1986, 4: *AAS* 78 (1986), 1120.

the victims of the most atrocious deaths to die again if we do not have an ardent desire for justice, if we do not commit ourselves to ensure that evil does not prevail over good as it did for millions of the children of the Jewish people....Humanity cannot permit all that to happen again".[22]

We pray that our sorrow for the tragedy which the Jewish people has suffered in our century will lead to a new relationship with the Jewish people. We wish to turn awareness of past sins into a firm resolve to build a new future in which there will be no more anti-Judaism among Christians or anti-Christian sentiment among Jews, but rather a shared mutual respect, as befits those who adore the one Creator and Lord and have a common father in faith, Abraham.

Finally, we invite all men and women of good will to reflect deeply on the significance of the *Shoah*. The victims from their graves, and the survivors through the vivid testimony of what they have suffered, have become a loud voice calling the attention of all humanity. To remember this terrible experience is to become fully conscious of the salutary warning it entails: the spoiled seeds of anti-Judaism and anti-Semitism must never again be allowed to take root in any human heart.

16 March 1998.

Cardinal Edward Idris Cassidy
President

The Most Reverend Pierre Duprey
Vice-President

The Reverend Remi Hoeckman, O.P.
Secretary

---

[22] Pope John Paul II, *Address on the occasion of a commemoration of the Shoah,* 7 April 1994, 3: *Insegnamenti* 17/1, 1994, 897 and 893.

Commentary by Rabbi Leon Klenicki

The Vatican Commission for Religious Relations with the Jews issued in Rome on March 16, 1998, a document called *We Remember: A Reflection on the* Shoah. It was presented by Edward Idris Cardinal Cassidy, head of the Holy See's commission. The twelve-page document deals with matters related to the Holocaust, the role of the church during that period, and the Catholic understanding of the Holocaust in Jewish and Christian history.

In 1987, Pope John Paul II promised at a Castel Gandolfo meeting with Jewish leadership a statement that would consider what role anti-Semitism and the church might have played in the Holocaust. The diabolic reality of the Holocaust has concerned him since his youth, when he witnessed the horror of the *Shoah* in his native Poland. This is evident in his letter to Cardinal Cassidy, introducing *We Remember,* where the pope says:

> On numerous occasions during my Pontificate I have recalled with a sense of deep sorrow the sufferings of the Jewish people during the Second World War. The crime which has become known as the *Shoah* remains an indelible stain on the history of the century that is coming to a close.

He adds that,

> As we prepare for the beginning of the Third Millennium of Christianity, the Church is aware that the joy of a Jubilee is above all the joy that is based on the forgiveness of sins and reconciliation with God and neighbour. Therefore, she encourages her sons and daughters to purify their hearts, through repentance of past errors and infidelities. She calls them to place themselves humbly before the Lord and examine themselves on the responsibility which they do have for the evils of our time.

Such a spirit should have been the inspiring source for a statement on the Holocaust. Pope John Paul II has denounced the horror of the *Shoah* often. He did it in Poland under Communist domination while visiting Auschwitz. The Polish government, influenced by Stalinist anti-Semitism, did not refer specifically to the killing of Jews but referred to all victims as Europeans. Pope John Paul II, at that time archbishop of Krakow, spoke clearly of the victims as part of the Jewish people.

John Paul II referred to the Holocaust in remarks to all European bishops and cardinals after the fall of Communism:

> The tragic series of events that have followed one after another during this century, particularly since the outbreak of the Second World War, have contributed perhaps in some measure to opening the human heart to the freedom which comes from the Spirit, that freedom by which Christ has set us free (cf. Galatians 5:1).
>
> The war itself with its immense cruelty, a cruelty that reached its most brutal expression in the organized extermination of the Jews, as well as of the Gypsies and of other categories of people, revealed to the European the other side of

a civilization that he was inclined to consider superior to all others. Certainly, the war also brought out people's readiness to show solidarity and make heroic sacrifices for a just cause. But these admirable aspects of the war experience seemed to be overwhelmed by the immensity of evil and destruction, not only on the material plane but also in the moral order. Perhaps in no other war in history has man been so thoroughly trampled upon in his dignity and fundamental rights. An echo of the humiliation and even desperation caused by such an experience could be heard in the question often repeated after the war: How can we go on living after Auschwitz? Sometimes another question presented itself: Is it still possible to speak about God after Auschwitz?[1]

John Paul II is hopeful that a joint Christian-Jewish reflection on the Shoah, its roots and ideology, would help to heal wounds of the past and become a reckoning of the soul for a joint witnessing of both faith commitments. He points out in his letter to Cardinal Cassidy, which introduces the Vatican document, that,

> It is my fervent hope that the document: *We Remember: A Reflection on the* Shoah, which the Commission for Religious Relations with the Jews has prepared under your direction, will indeed help to heal the wounds of past mis-understandings and injustices. May it enable memory to play its necessary part in the process of shaping a future in which the unspeakable iniquity of the *Shoah* will never again be possible. May the Lord of history guide the efforts of Catholics and Jews and all men and women of good will as they work together for a world of true respect for the life and dignity of every human being, for all have been created in the image and likeness of God.

We Remember reflects partially the hopeful thought of Pope John Paul II. But some sections of the Vatican document express concepts that are of serious concern in a Jewish reading that in turn reflects the author's own Jewish religious commitment, vocation for Catholic-Jewish dialogue, and respect for the Catholic tradition. This essay also tries to convey a personal committed Jewish religious wish to share the pain of history, the *Shoah*, and the yearning for a joint Christian-Jewish testimony, responding together to the possibilities of human evil and the ever-present scourge of anti-Semitism and racism in any of its manifestations.

The following comments focus on each consecutive section of *We Remember.*

I. THE TRAGEDY OF THE *SHOAH* AND THE DUTY OF REMEMBRANCE

The first section invites all men and women to think and react to what happened in the twentieth century, and especially in this indescribable evil of the Holocaust. The *Shoah* is described as

> an unspeakable tragedy, which can never be forgotten: the attempt by the Nazi regime to exterminate the Jewish people, with the consequent killing of millions of Jews. Women and men, old and young, children and infants, for the sole reason of their Jewish origin, were persecuted and deported. Some were killed immediately, while others were degraded, illtreated, tortured and utterly robbed of their human dignity, and then murdered. Very few of those who entered the Camps survived, and those who did remain scarred for life. This was the *Shoah*. It is a major fact of the history of this century, a fact which still concerns us today.

This is an important statement reminding humanity of the diabolic reality of the Holocaust in the twentieth century. It is a clear and strong response to those who deny the *Shoah*. The Vatican document points this out to all members of the Catholic Church and to humanity, asking all to reflect on the "catastrophe which befell the Jewish people, and on the moral imperative to ensure that never again will selfishness and hatred grow to the point of sowing with suffering and death."

The document asks Jewish friends "to hear us with open hearts." This is a cordial and welcome invitation. The Jewish readers and the Jewish people are hearing the voice of the official church, something new in the stormy relationship between Christians and Jews. It is an invitation to a dialogue and encounter, accepting each other as members of God's people, yet aware of spiritual differences. As a listener, the Jew has the obligation to hear but also to respond in a committed manner, aware of past and present historical and religious experiences, while avoiding any form of triumphalism. Otherwise, such a dialogue is really only an exchange of monologues.

II. WHAT WE MUST REMEMBER

Then the document invites Christians to "a very serious reflection on what gave rise" to the *Shoah*. *We Remember* stresses the fact that the *Shoah* took place in Europe, "that is, in countries of long-standing Christian civilization" and points out that the geography of the Holocaust "raises the question of the relation between the Nazi persecution and the attitude down the centuries of Christians toward the Jews." This is an excellent proposition, though a more detailed explanation focusing on the social and theological measures taken by the church and Christian leadership in the process of alienation and persecution of Jews in Europe has been urgently sought for many years.

In *We Remember* there is no criticism of church leadership, clerical or lay, for the degree of blame assumed for the racial transgressions of Catholics and for inculcating inadequate theological notions that denied any significance to Judaism and the Jewish people in God's design following the death of Jesus. Would this not be the time to express sorrow for past episcopal legislation against the Jews, similar in many respects to that enacted by the Nazi regime?

The historian Raul Hilberg lists twenty-two conciliar or synodal decrees that were restrictive of Jews from the fourth to the fifteenth centuries and were paralleled by specific Nazi decrees. He lists them as follows:

1) Prohibition of intermarriage and of sexual intercourse between Christians and Jews, Synod of Elvira, A.D. 306.

2) Jews and Christians not permitted to eat together, Synod of Elvira.

3) Jews not allowed to hold public office, Synod of Clermont, A.D. 535.

4) Jews not allowed to employ Christian servants or possess Christian slaves, 3rd Synod of Orleans, A.D. 538.

5) Jews not permitted to show themselves in the streets during Passion Week, 3rd Synod of Orleans.

6) Burning of the Talmud and other books, 12th Synod of Toledo, A.D. 681.

7) Christians not permitted to patronize Jewish doctors, Trullanic Synod, A.D. 692.

8) Christians not permitted to live in Jewish homes, Synod Narbonne, A.D.. 1050.

9) Jews obliged to pay taxes for support of the Church to the same extent as Christians, Synod of Gerona, A.D. 1078.

10) Prohibition of Sunday work by Jews, Synod of Szabolcs, A.D. 1092.

11) Jews not permitted to be plaintiffs, or witnesses against Christians in the courts, 3rd Lateran Council, A.D. 1179, Canon 26.

12) Jews not permitted to withhold inheritance from descendants who had accepted Christianity, 3rd Lateran Council, Canon 26.

13) The marking of Jewish clothes with a badge, 4th Lateran Council, A.D.. 1215, Canon 68 (copied from the legislation by Caliph Omar II, A.D. 643–44, who had decreed that Christians wear blue belts and Jews yellow belts).

14) Construction of new synagogues prohibited, Council of Oxford, A.D. 1222.

15) Christians not permitted to attend Jewish ceremonies, Synod of Vienna, A.D. 1267.

16) Jews not permitted to dispute with simple Christian people about the tenets of the Catholic religion, Synod of Vienna.

17) Compulsory ghettos, Synod of Breslau, A.D.. 1227.

18) Christians not permitted to sell or rent real estate to Jews, Synod of Ofen, A.D. 1279.

19) Adoption by a Christian of the Jewish religion or return by a baptized Jew to the Jewish religion defined as heresy, Synod of Mainz, A.D.. 1310.

20) Sale or transfer of Church articles to Jews prohibited, Synod of Lavour, A.D. 1368.

21) Jews not permitted to act as agents in the conclusion of contracts between Christians, especially marriage contracts, Council of Basel, A.D. 1432, Sessio XIX.

22) Jews not permitted to obtain academic degrees, Council of Basel, Sessio XIX.[2]

It is essential, therefore, that we acknowledge a continuity in the persecutions against Jews from the Constantinian period in the fourth century, all the way to the present day. The fact that the *Shoah* took place in Europe,

the heart of Christianity, requires a reckoning of the soul!
Indeed, it needs a joint Christian-Jewish reckoning that
would help interfaith healing, facing together the challenge
imposed by almost limitless human evil.

III. RELATIONS BETWEEN JEWS
AND CHRISTIANS

We Remember recognizes that "the balance of these
relations over two thousand years has been quite negative."
Vatican Council II, however, opened new possibilities and
perspectives in the relationship of Catholics and Jews by
accepting the Jewish people as a subject of faith with its
own religious legitimacy, by denouncing the deicide accusation, and by recommending changes in preaching and
teaching to overcome any form of theological anti-Jewish
prejudice.

We Remember seems at times to overlook this very
process of clarification mandated by Vatican Council II.

The third section of the document, for example, is
devoted to a short history of the relationship of Jews and
Christians through the centuries. It talks about the confrontation of the first century between Jews and the early
Christian community. The text stresses that "the Jewish
leaders and people, in their devotion to the Law, on occasion violently opposed the preachers of the Gospel and the
first Christians." Was the Law the only "devotion" of the
Jewish people? Was it *just* a devotion to the Law that led to
the opposition to the preachers of the gospel? The diverse
groups within the Jewish people—Sadducees, Pharisees,
Essenes, and others—which reflected the social and spiritual pluralism of the Jewish people at the time, were divided

in their interpretation of God's Word and will. This was the major focus of their internal conflicts and would eventually affect their view of Christians and their brethren who opposed the Jews. To characterize this position as simply the result of the latter's devotion to "Law" is to misrepresent the spiritual life of the Jews both then and since. It is disturbing to see this stereotype of the Jewish people as one bound by the Law. Surely, this is a misunderstanding that polemically contrasts Law and Love and reminds the reader of stereotypes typical of pre–Vatican II dialogue.

Was the confrontation of Jews and early Christians different from other discussions in the first century? Not at all, and this can be seen in rabbinical texts that testify to the pluralism of the time. There was no central authority or magisterium to decide on such disputes. Theological confrontation was a daily reality in the first century. *We Remember* points out the "violence" perpetrated by rabbinic Jews against the followers of Jesus. The text seems to indicate that Jews treated Christians badly, though there is no evidence of forced separation or the obligation of wearing symbols on clothing denouncing a Christian commitment. First-century Jews did not create ghettos for the followers of Christ. The theological opposition between Jews of any position and early Christians was a common event following the religious pluralism of the first century. The centuries that followed would show a different view in detriment of Jews and Judaism.

A new chapter began in the relationship between Christians and Jews after the recognition of Christianity as the official religion of the Roman Empire by Constantine. From that moment on, Jews were separated from society, confronted theologically, and forbidden to preach their own commitment to the community at large. This is clearly described in *We Remember,* recognizing medieval Christian contempt for Jews and Judaism:

> Despite the Christian preaching of love for all, even for one's enemies, the prevailing mentality down the centuries penalized minorities and those who were in any way "different." Sentiments of anti-Judaism in some Christian quarters, and the gap which existed between the Church and the Jewish people, led to a generalized discrimination, which ended at times in expulsions or attempts at forced conversions. In a large part of the "Christian" world, until the end of the 18th century, those who were not Christian did not always enjoy a fully guaranteed juridical status. Despite that fact, Jews throughout Christendom held on to their religious traditions and communal customs. They were therefore looked upon with a certain suspicion and mistrust. In times of crisis such as famine, war, pestilence or social tensions, the Jewish minority was sometimes taken as a scapegoat and became the victim of violence, looting, even massacres.

Section III refers to Nazi Germany, noting that "the Church in Germany replied by condemning racism. The condemnation first appeared in the preaching of some of the clergy, in the public teaching of the Catholic Bishops, and in the writings of lay Catholic journalists." Unfortunately, the personal denunciations of some cardinals or lay leadership didn't become the official position of the Catholic Church in Germany. A statement by the German and Austrian bishops' conferences on the occasion of the fiftieth anniversary of the liberation of the Auschwitz concentration camp painfully stated:

> Today the fact is weighing heavily on our mind that individual initiatives to help persecuted Jews and that even the

pogroms of November 1938 were not followed by public and expressed protests; i.e., when hundreds of synagogues were set on fire and vandalized, cemeteries were desecrated, thousands of Jewish-owned shops were demolished, innumerable dwellings of Jewish families were damaged and looted, people were ridiculed, ill-treated and even killed.

The German episcopal conference document stresses that

the retrospect of the events of November 1938 and on the terror regime of the National Socialists during twelve years visualizes the heavy burden of history. It records "that the Church, which we proclaim as holy and which we all know as a mystery, is also a sinful church and in need of conversion."

It would have been a significant contribution of the Holy See's own document to include this quotation from the German bishops, as well as quotations from the French bishops' "Declaration of Repentance," confessing a sad moment of Christian indifference in a Europe dominated by a paganism that was destroying the Jewish people. If the German bishops were able to stop the Nazi murder of incapacitated children in the late 1930s by their outspoken intervention, then doesn't it stand to reason that a Christian condemnation of Nazism and its anti-Semitism would have saved Jewish lives or stopped the *Shoah?* Instead, there was silence for the Jewish situation even in the wake of *Kristallnacht* and the pogroms of November 1938, when synagogues and Jewish community buildings were set on fire.

IV. NAZI ANTI-SEMITISM AND THE *SHOAH*

The Vatican document points out the difference between anti-Semitism and anti-Judaism. While anti-Semitism is the denial of Jewish existence focusing on social alienation or destruction of the Jewish community, anti-Judaism is the theological denial of Judaism. The anti-Judaism that the text acknowledges, of which "unfortunately, Christians also have been guilty," is not described; instead, it is taken for granted that the reader will understand all the relevant connotations. It is unfortunate that no references were included here to the meeting Anti-Judaism in the Christian Milieu, called by Pope John Paul II, who is well aware of the theological methodology in the use and abuse of New Testament texts that denigrate Judaism. He convoked this gathering of sixty scholars on October 31–November 1, 1997, to consider the Christian roots of anti-Judaism. Pope John Paul II said in his welcoming speech to all present that "erroneous and unjust interpretations of the New Testament regarding the Jewish people and their presumed guilt circulated for too long" and "contributed to a lulling of many consciences" at the time of World War II. He stressed that while there were "Christians who did everything to save those who were persecuted, even to the point of risking their own lives, the spiritual resistance of many was not what humanity expected of Christ's disciples."[3]

It is sad that section IV of *We Remember*, recognizing the influence of anti-Judaism in Christian theology, wasn't developed more thoroughly. It should have clarified what was meant by saying that "the *Shoah* was the work of a thoroughly modern neo-pagan regime. Its anti-Semitism had its roots outside of Christianity and, in pursuing its aims, it did not hesitate to oppose the Church and persecute her members also."

This statement requires careful reflection. It is highly optimistic of the document to say that the anti-Semitism of Nazi ideology had its roots outside of Christianity. By doing so, it denies centuries of Christian contempt and persecution of Jews and Judaism. It should be remembered that anti-Judaism created the atmosphere for the possibility of pagan anti-Semitism. This same point was already made by Jules Isaac in his book *The Teaching of Contempt: Christian Roots of Anti-Semitism,* which deeply influenced Pope John XXIII in his decision to prepare a document on the relationship of the Catholic Church to Judaism. Professor Isaac shared in this classic work that the teaching of contempt molded generations of Christians in their anti-Jewish feeling. His thought can be appreciated in the following paragraph of *We Remember,*

> But it may be asked whether the Nazi persecution of the Jews was not made easier by the anti-Jewish prejudice imbedded in some Christian minds and hearts. Did anti-Jewish sentiment among Christians make them less sensitive, or even indifferent, to the persecutions launched against the Jews by National Socialism?

A document such as this, which raises questions about past and even present negative stands on Judaism and the Jewish people, has a religious and moral duty to show how much the teaching of contempt has influenced Christianity throughout the centuries and how it deeply affected the Christian responses to Nazi persecution. *We Remember* would have been more effective if it had helped Catholics to understand the nature of theological contempt for Judaism still present in preaching and teaching of the pre-war period. The teaching of contempt, that is, theological anti-Judaism, is generally not separated from anti-Semitism. Nazi propaganda historically used the theological anti-Judaism of Catholic theologians and religious art to back its racist ideology. Anti-Judaism, present in European culture, art, the vitraux of many cathedrals, and Western literature, paved the way for the "neo-pagan" anti-Semitism of Nazism. Sadly, this cultural and theological heritage is still a reality in the collective unconscious of the West.

Christian prayers, especially the Passion Week liturgy, have projected an anti-Judaism that nurtured the anti-Semitism of centuries. Pope John Paul II, aware of this matter, took a clarifying step forward in the liturgy of 1998's Good Friday "Via Crucis." Lisa Palmieri-Billig describes the ceremony in a report,

> During his traditional Good Friday "Via Crucis" procession from the Colosseum to the Roman Forum on Friday evening, Pope John Paul II said that "not the Jewish people, which has been crucified by us for too long...but we, each and every one of us" are responsible for Christ's crucifixion.
>
> He said, "That cry of death, 'Crucify him,' resounds throughout history and the century now ending...the ashes of Auschwitz and the ice of the Gulag, water and blood of the Asian rice fields, the lakes of Africa, murdered paradises, so many children denied, prostituted, mutilated...." The responsibility "for that cry of death is not the Jewish people—too long crucified by us; not they, but we, each and every one of us, because we are all assassins of love."
>
> The Pope's words were written by Olivier Clement, a French Orthodox theologian, at the Pope's special request. The Pontiff's desire for a reflection on the Church's past errors and Christian sins throughout history is a stated part

of the "purification process" which he has repeatedly called for, leading to the Jubilee Year. "We Remember: Reflections on the Shoah" is an important step in that process.

This "mea culpa" recurred several times during the observance of the day. During the liturgy in the Vatican Basilica over which the Pope presided, Reverend Raniero Cantalamessa, the apostolic preacher, said "It is just that we start this process on Good Friday." The Pope and the entire Roman Curia listened as Cantalamessa told them that the Church Fathers of the Second Century "sowed the seeds" of anti-Judaism and "indirectly favored the Shoah."

It is the first time in history that such statements have been made on Good Friday and with the blessing of the Pope himself. Though similar thoughts were expressed already in the "Roman Catechism" of the Council of Trent, they were not applied, and never stated with such force and depth of feeling, moreover during the Easter triduum.

Good Friday has traditionally been a time of fear for Jews, when anti-Jewish preaching incited crowds to hatred and often to violence as well. John XXIII was the first Pope to lead Catholics towards a new theology of Jews, when he removed the words "perfidious Jews" from Good Friday prayers. Now, decades later, after a long, ongoing process of Catholic-Jewish dialogue, a new step, light years ahead of the first, has been taken.[4]

Section IV devotes much attention to papal attitudes toward European totalitarianism. Pius XI denounced the totalitarian nature of Nazism, as did Pius XII, but did not mention the direct persecution of Jews or the Christian past that facilitated Nazi persecution. *We Remember* states that,

> Pope Pius XI too condemned Nazi racism in a solemn way in his Encyclical Letter *Mit brennender Sorge,* which was read in German churches on Passion Sunday 1937, a step which resulted in attacks and sanctions against members of the clergy. Addressing a group of Belgian pilgrims on 6

September 1938, Pius XI asserted: "Anti-Semitism is unacceptable. Spiritually, we are all Semites." Pius XII, in his very first Encyclical, *Summi Pontificatus*, of 20 October 1939, warned against theories which denied the unity of the human race and against the deification of the State, all of which he saw as leading to a real "hour of darkness."

A whole paragraph of the document is devoted to the fact that some Western countries of Christian tradition in North and South America "were more than hesitant to open the borders to the persecuted Jews." This is true and painful. "The closing of borders to Jewish emigration in those circumstances, whether due to anti-Jewish hostility or suspicion, political cowardice or shortsightedness, or national selfishness, lays a heavy burden of conscience on the authorities in question." It would have been very important at that time—in fact, crucial—when so many doors were closed to Jews, for Pope Pius XII openly to condemn Nazi anti-Semitism and deny and denounce the "final solution." His condemnation would have opened the doors for Jewish refugees to many countries, especially in Catholic Latin America.

The document quotes from the Second Vatican Council declaration *Nostra Aetate,* which affirms: "The Church...mindful of her common patrimony with the Jews, and motivated by the Gospel's spiritual love and by no political considerations, deplores the hatred, persecutions and displays of anti-Semitism directed against the Jews at any time and from any source." *The Vatican Guidelines and Suggestions for Implementing the Conciliatory Declaration* Nostra Aetate *(No. 4),* December 4, 1974, points out that,

the step taken by the Council finds its historical setting and circumstances deeply affected by the memory of the persecution and massacre of Jews which took place in Europe before and during the Second World War....While referring the reader back to this document (*Nostra Aetate*), we may simply restate here that the spiritual bonds and historical links binding the Church to Judaism condemn as opposed to the very spirit of Christianity all forms of anti-Semitism and discrimination which in any case the dignity of the human person alone would suffice to condemn.

The language of condemnation found in the Vatican *Guidelines* would have better served *We Remember* than the less challenging phrase "deplores" found in *Nostra Aetate.*

It is important to point out that the Commission for Justice and Peace, which issued *The Church and Racism* on November 3, 1988, outlined the church's condemnation of anti-Semitism as well as its concern about the use of anti-Zionism as a form of anti-Semitism. The paragraph states:

Amongst the manifestations of systematic racial distrust, specific mention must once again be made of *anti-Semitism.* If anti-Semitism has been the most tragic form that racist ideology has assumed in our century, with the horrors of the Jewish "holocaust," it has unfortunately not yet entirely disappeared. As if some had nothing to learn from the crimes of the past, certain organizations, with branches in many countries, keep alive the anti-Semite racist myth, with the support of networks of publications. Terrorist acts which have Jewish persons or symbols as their target have multiplied in recent years and show the radicalism of such groups. Anti-Zionism—which is not of the same order, since it questions the State of Israel and its policies—serves at a time as a screen for anti-Semitism, feeding on it and leading to it. Furthermore, some countries impose undue harassments and restrictions on the free emigration of Jews.[5]

We Remember reproduces Pope John Paul II's address to the leaders of the Jewish community in Strasbourg in

1988, where he stated: "I repeat again with you the strongest condemnation of anti-Semitism and racism, which are opposed to the principles of Christianity." Once again, it is John Paul II who provides the strongest and most effective language defining anti-Semitism as a sin.

The final part of the last paragraph of section IV is devoted to other forms of persecution and genocide in this century. The text says:

> We recall in particular the massacre of the Armenians, the countless victims in Ukraine in the 1930s, the genocide of the Gypsies which was also the result of racist ideas, and similar tragedies which have occurred in America, Africa, and the Balkans. Nor do we forget the millions of victims of totalitarian ideology in the Soviet Union, in China, Cambodia and elsewhere. Nor can we forget the drama of the Middle East, the elements of which are well known. Even as we make this reflection, "many human beings are still their brothers' victims."

Are we to think that this reference to other forms of genocide in the world equalizes them with the Nazi Holocaust? Catholic belief clearly links the salvation of Christians with God's redemption of the Jewish people, whose covenant with God is irrevocable, as Paul made clear in his Letter to the Romans. Can Christians view the *Shoah* in the same way as they do other genocides? Further, the reference to the Middle East—made without further clarification—seems rather inappropriate at the end of a list of the massacres of our century. What are the "elements" referred to here?

Equating other genocides with the Holocaust contradicts what Pope John Paul II said previously, for example, at the Holocaust Concert or in his address on the occasion of the Commemoration of the *Shoah,* April 7, 1994:

> We would risk causing the victims of the most atrocious death to die again if we do not have an ardent desire for justice, if we do not commit ourselves to ensure that evil does not prevail over good as it did for millions of the children of the Jewish people…humanity cannot permit all that to happen again.

V. LOOKING TOGETHER TO A COMMON FUTURE

The last section of the document reminds its readers of the close relationship of Christianity to Judaism and that "the Jews are our dearly beloved brothers, indeed in a certain sense they are 'our elder brothers,'" repeating what Pope John Paul II said in his speech at the Synagogue of Rome, April 13, 1986.

We Remember expresses repentance (*teshuva*), that is, a call to the conscience of humanity:

> At the end of the Millennium the Catholic Church desires to express her deep sorrow for the failures of her sons and daughters in every age. This is an act of repentance (*teshuva*), since, as members of the Church, we are linked to the sins as well as the merits of all her children. The Church approaches with deep respect and great compassion the experience of extermination, the *Shoah,* suffered by the Jewish people during World War II. It is not a matter of mere words, but indeed of binding commitment.

We wholeheartedly agree with *We Remember* that, as we begin a new Christian millennium, we need to reflect together on the unique significance of the *Shoah* and its total horror, which remind humanity of the unlimited possibilities of human evil. We are hopeful that Christian repentance for centuries of persecution and mistreatment of Jews and Judaism

> will lead to a new relationship with the Jewish people. We wish to turn awareness of past sins into a firm resolve to build a new future in which there will be no more anti-Judaism among Christians or anti-Christian sentiment among Jews, but rather a shared mutual respect, as befits those who adore the one Creator and Lord and have a common father in faith, Abraham.

Sadly confounding is the reference to "anti-Christian sentiment among Jews." Perhaps there is such a sentiment, but is it not likely that in many cases it is a response to centuries of Christian contempt toward Judaism? However, even in its most virulent forms, it has never produced Jewish Crusades, persecutions, discrimination, and even murder of whole Christian communities, as was done in Christian Europe against the Jews or in the Christian silence over Auschwitz, the symbol of the *Shoah*.

A FINAL REFLECTION

We Remember: A Reflection on the Shoah is a disappointment to the Jewish community, which waited eleven years for this document. So much progress had been made in Catholic-Jewish relations since the historic Vatican II *Nostra Aetate* document that when word came that the Vatican was going to issue a major document on the church and the Holocaust, expectations rose that the new document would respond to Jewish pain, offering a Christian reckoning of the soul to the presence of the total evil of the Holocaust experience. Pope John Paul II has personally taken many important steps to announce the church's greater sensitivity to the Jewish people. Whether it was his visit to the Synagogue in Rome, the first such visit ever by a pontiff, or establishing diplomatic relations with the State of Israel, condemning anti-Semitism as a sin, or declaring the innate legitimacy of Judaism as a brother and sister religion to Christianity, his messages were positive and hopeful.

Moreover, in recent months, the bishops of Germany and France had shown greater Catholic sensitivity to the evils of the past in their respective documents. It is in this context that the Vatican document on the Holocaust is so disappointing. Unlike the French and German statements, the Holy See specifically rejected a connection between the Holocaust and Christianity. It called the Holocaust the "work of a thoroughly modern neo-pagan regime" and added that its "anti-Semitism had its roots outside of Christianity." This notion belies the history of Christian anti-Semitism, which for centuries suffused Europe with hatred and contempt for Judaism, while creating an environment that made the Holocaust possible. It undermines the major effort of so much interfaith dialogue in recent years that focuses on the disastrous consequences of delegitimizing another people and another religion. As was mentioned above, it was Pope John Paul II himself who convened an international meeting of Catholic scholars in October 1997 to consider the serious matter of anti-Judaism in the teaching and preaching of the church.

The role of Pius XII is presented in favorable fashion but ignores the many opportunities that he had as a world religious leader to help stop the slaughter of the Jews. The defense of Pius XII in the document reinforces Jewish belief that it is crucial that the church open all of its archives for research and investigation. Only these files can clarify and complete the picture of the pope's policy and conduct during the war.

Unlike the German and French documents, in which those who stood up and rescued Jews were seen as exceptions, the Vatican document gives the impression that those who were evil, insensitive, and acquiesced to the "final solution," were exceptions to the overall Christian approach.

In truth, had this Vatican document appeared before *Nostra Aetate,* before the succession of remarkable steps taken by John Paul II, before the French and German bishops' statements, one might have termed it courageous for even looking at the church's role during the Jewish tragedy and for its denunciation of anti-Semitism. But the document was issued in 1998, two years before the millennium. It was hoped that *We Remember* would culminate in the process of reconciliation between Christianity and Judaism that previous efforts had helped to create. Regrettably, it has done exactly the opposite.

PERSONAL REFLECTION

Disappointed as we are, we remain nevertheless committed to continuing the creative interfaith dialogue, a call of God, that projects a message of hope to humanity. We share wholeheartedly the final message of the document. Let us reflect together at the beginning of the third Christian millennium:

Finally, we invite all men and women of good will to reflect deeply on the significance of the *Shoah*. The victims from their graves, and the survivors through the vivid testimony of what they have suffered, have become a loud voice calling the attention of all of humanity. To remember this terrible experience is to become fully conscious of the salutary warning it entails: the spoiled seeds of anti-Judaism and anti-Semitism must never again be allowed to take root in any human heart.

NOTES

1. Pope John Paul II, *Spiritual Pilgrimage: Texts on Jews and Judaism, 1979–1995,* ed. with com. and intro. Eugene J. Fisher and Leon Klenicki (New York: Crossroad, 1995).

2. Raul Hilberg, *The Destruction of the European Jews* (Chicago: Quadrangle Books, 1961), 5f.

3. Pope John Paul II, an address to participants at the symposium "The Roots of Anti-Judaism in the Christian Milieu," *Origins* 27, no. 22 (November 13, 1997).

4. Lisa Palmieri-Billig, "Pope Speaks Out Against Deicide Accusation," a report (Rome, April 11, 1998).

5. *Anti-Semitism Is a Sin* (a discussion of the document *The Church and Racism: Towards a More Fraternal Society*), ed. Eugene J. Fisher and Leon Klenicki (New York: Anti-Defamation League, 1994).

Commentary by Avery Dulles, S.J.

HISTORICAL BACKGROUND

The *Declaration on the Relationship of the Church to Non-Christian Religions (Nostra Aetate)* issued by the Second Vatican Council in 1965 inaugurated a new era of Jewish-Catholic relations based on cordiality and trust. In two key paragraphs it stated:

> True, authorities of the Jews and those who followed their lead pressed for the death of Christ (cf. Jn 19:6); still, what happened in His passion cannot be blamed upon all the Jews then living, without distinction, nor upon the Jews of today. Although the Church is the new people of God, the Jews should not be presented as repudiated or cursed by God, as if such views followed from the holy Scriptures. All should take pains, then, lest in catechetical instruction and in the preaching of God's Word they teach anything out of harmony with the truth of the gospel and the spirit of Christ.
>
> The Church repudiates all persecutions against any man. Moreover, mindful of her common patrimony with the Jews, and motivated by the gospel's spiritual love and by no political considerations, she deplores the hatred, persecutions, and displays of anti-Semitism directed against the Jews at any time and from any source.[1]

47

This declaration was a great advance over any previous Church document on the subject of Jewish-Catholic relations, though it drew upon earlier statements such as those of Pius XI and Pius XII. The Jews expressed general satisfaction, but on some counts many of them were disappointed. They would have liked to see some indication of sorrow and repentance for the mistreatment of Jews by Catholics in the past. They were also displeased by two changes in the wording of the definitive version. Whereas a previous draft had denied that the Jews were guilty of deicide, the final text omitted the word "deicide"—a term that according to many theologians ought to be banished from Christian vocabulary. And whereas a previous draft had not only "deplored" but also "condemned" anti-Semitism, the term "condemn" was dropped in the final version, possibly on the ground that Pope John XXIII had asked the council to refrain from condemnations. These two changes were perceived by many as dilutions.

In the years following Vatican II, Catholic-Jewish relations from the Catholic side continued to be handled, as they had been since 1959, by a special desk within the Secretariat for Promoting Christian Unity (SPCU). In 1970 the SPCU, together with the International Jewish Committee on Interreligious Consultations, established a Catholic/Jewish International Liaison Committee, which has since been holding annual meetings.

The document *We Remember* emanates from the Commission for Religious Relations with the Jews and is signed by its current president, Cardinal Edward I. Cassidy. This commission is a separate body, set up by Pope Paul VI in 1974, but the president of the secretariat (now known as the Pontifical Council for Christian Unity) is ex officio its president. The commission issued in 1975 a document, *Guidelines on Religious Relations with the Jews,* that suggested ways of implementing the council's declaration in dialogue, liturgy, religious education, and joint social action. Restoring the word that had been deleted from the conciliar text, the *Guidelines* said emphatically that all forms of anti-Semitism are to be "condemned."[2]

In 1985 the commission published *Notes on the Correct Way to Present the Jews and Judaism in Preaching and Catechesis.*[3] Touching on the Holocaust, the *Notes* said simply that "catechesis should...help in understanding the meaning for the Jews of the extermination during the years 1939–1945, and its consequences" (§25). Strangely, nothing was included about the meaning of the Holocaust for Christians.

In the late summer of 1987, after the welcome given to Kurt Waldheim at the Vatican had raised tensions between the Holy See and the Jewish community, a meeting was held at Rome with representatives of the International Jewish Committee on Interreligious Consultations. At that meeting Cardinal Jan Willebrands, then president of the secretariat, announced that the Commission for Religious Relations with the Jews intended to prepare a statement on the Holocaust. Speaking to Jewish leaders at Castel Gandolfo on September 1, 1987, the pope confirmed that the document would be forthcoming.

The production of the commission's document was delayed several years, partly because many of the national conferences of Catholic bishops intended to issue their own statements on the Holocaust (or, as many prefer to say, the *Shoah*).[4] Rome did not wish to speak until these regional bodies had had their say. The Hungarian bishops led with an ecumenical statement of October 26, 1992.

The fiftieth anniversary of the liberation of Auschwitz (January 27, 1945) occasioned statements by a number of conferences: the German bishops (January 17, 1995), the Polish bishops (January 27, 1995), and the United States bishops (January 27, 1995). This last statement was actually signed by Archbishop Oscar Lipscomb as chairman of the Bishops' Committee for Ecumenical and Interreligious Affairs. The Dutch bishops released a statement in October 1995. The Swiss bishops expressed themselves in a letter to the Italian Jewish community on March 16, 1997. After a group of French bishops spoke up on September 30, 1997, the way was clear for the Holy See to make a pronouncement on behalf of the universal church.

Several of these national statements contained notable expressions of contrition. The German bishops, quoting from their own joint synod of 1975, declared:

> In this period of National Socialism—despite the exemplary behavior of some individuals and groups—we were nevertheless, as a whole, a church community who kept on living their life in turning their back too often on the fate of this persecuted Jewish people, who looked too fixedly at the threat to their own institutions and who remained silent about the crimes committed against the Jews and Judaism.[5]

The Polish bishops, in their statement of January 1995, remarked that the creators of Auschwitz were not Poles but Nazi Germans, but at the same time they quoted from their previous pastoral letter of 1991: "In spite of numerous heroic examples of Polish Christians, there were those who remained indifferent to that inconceivable tragedy. In particular, we mourn the fact that there were also those among Catholics who in some way had contributed to the death of Jews. They will forever remain a source of remorse in the social dimension."[6]

Archbishop Lipscomb, in his January 1995 statement on behalf of the United States bishops, recalled with regret and humility the refusal of the United States to accept Jewish refugees during the war. He also deplored the failure of Americans to bomb the railroad lines leading to Auschwitz, as Jewish leaders had besought them to do. Lipscomb's statement acknowledged a sense of responsibility for the failures of fellow-Catholics in Europe to do everything possible to save Jewish lives.[7]

The Swiss bishops in March 1997 confessed that religious motivations played a part in the atrocities committed during the Hitler years and proclaimed that although these unworthy motivations "are today largely incomprehensible," Christians must acknowledge their culpability and ask pardon from the descendants of the victims.[8]

The most dramatic act of repentance thus far is the French statement of September 1997. A group of bishops, including Cardinal Jean-Marie Lustiger of Paris, gathered at Drancy, the site of a former Jewish concentration camp. They lamented the failure of the bishops of France to issue public statements against the internment camps and deportations of Jews, at least until 1942, when some bishops in southern France courageously protested. They faulted the hierarchy for having concentrated too narrowly on the protection of the Catholic faithful and for succumbing to fear of reprisals against the church's activities and youth movements. In spite of commendable exceptions, said the bishops, "we must recognize that indifference won the day over indignation in the face of persecution of the Jews and that, in particular, silence was the rule in the face of the multifarious laws enacted by the Vichy government....We confess this sin. We beg God's pardon, and we call upon the Jewish people to hear our words of repentance."[9]

These national statements reflect the different experiences and involvements of the local churches in the events of the Nazi period. All of them, in their unity and variety, must be seen as belonging to the context of the present statement from the Holy See. The Vatican commission did not find it necessary to repeat everything that had been said by the particular bishops' conferences. Supplementing what had been said, the Holy See aimed to bring out what pertained to the universal church in pondering her own mystery and her relation to the Jewish people.

VIEWS OF JOHN PAUL II

The tragedy of the *Shoah* looms large in the consciousness of Pope John Paul II. He recalls that at least a fourth of the students in his elementary school at Wadowice were Jewish. In 1989, after he became pope, he commissioned one of these Jewish fellow-students, Jerzy Kluger, to bring a letter from him to the citizens of Wadowice for the unveiling of a commemorative plaque at the place where the synagogue had stood, honoring the Jews who had died in the *Shoah*, including all the members of Kluger's family who had remained in that town.[10] Kluger, as a lifelong friend of the pope, served as an unofficial go-between in the negotiations for the recognition of the State of Israel by the Holy See.[11]

The death chambers of Auschwitz stand out for John Paul II as the most meaningful symbol of the scourge of anti-Semitism. When he visited Auschwitz on June 7, 1979, he courteously refrained from interpreting what the Jewish people had there suffered in terms of Christian redemptive categories. He knelt in solemn commemoration before the inscriptions in twenty languages and paused especially at the inscription in Hebrew. Later that day, in a homily at Birkenau, he said:

> This inscription awakens the memory of the people whose sons and daughters were intended for total extermination. This people draws its origin from Abraham, our father in faith (cf. Rom 4:12), as was expressed by Paul of Tarsus. The very people who received from God the commandment "Thou shalt not kill," itself experienced in a special manner what is meant by killing. It is not permissible for anyone to pass by this inscription with indifference.[12]

According to the pope's biographer, George H. Williams, "Jews editorially and in conversation testify that the Pope conducted himself [on this occasion] with extraordinary tact, fellow feeling, and interfaith sensitivity."[13]

At a memorable visit to the synagogue in Rome on April 13, 1986, John Paul II spoke of the Jews as "our elder brothers in the faith" and once again expressed his "abhorrence for the genocide decreed against the Jewish people during the last war, which led to the holocaust of millions of innocent victims."[14] Addressing leaders of the Jewish community in Strasbourg in 1988, the pope said: "I repeat again with you the strongest condemnation of anti-Semitism and racism, which are opposed to the principles of Christianity."[15] At St. Peter's Square on April 18, 1993, John Paul II recalled the fiftieth anniversary of the uprising in the Warsaw ghetto. He spoke of the *Shoah* as "a true night of history, with unimaginable crimes against God and humanity."[16]

Thus far, the pope has been reserved in assigning blame to Christians and Catholics with regard to the Holocaust, though sometimes he seems to move in the direction of a confession of guilt. For example, in a letter of August 1, 1987, to the president of the United States Bishops' Conference, he wrote: "There is no doubt that the sufferings endured by the Jews are also for the Catholic Church a motive of sincere sorrow, especially when one thinks of the indifference and sometimes resentment which, in particular historical circumstances, have divided Jews and Christians."[17] Even more significantly, he recited the following prayer at an ecumenical service on December 7, 1991, at St. Peter's in the course of the European bishops' synod:

> Lord, our Liberator, we of the Christian communities of Europe have not always obeyed your precept but, relying only on human power, we have followed worldly prudence with wars of religion, with struggles of Christians against Christians, with indifference in the face of persecutions and the Holocaust of the Jews, with furious attacks against so many of the just. Pardon us and have mercy on us![18]

Still another conditioning factor needs to be kept in mind to situate the document *We Remember* in its proper framework. In 1994 Pope John Paul II called for a collective examination of conscience on the part of the church as part of its preparation for the Great Jubilee of the year 2000. "The Church," he wrote,

> cannot cross the threshold of the new millennium without encouraging her children to purify themselves, through repentance, of past errors and instances of infidelity, inconsistency, and slowness to act. Acknowledging the weaknesses of the past is an act of honesty and courage which

helps us to strengthen our faith, which alerts us to face today's temptations and challenges and prepares us to meet them.[19]

To implement this program the Holy See has established a number of committees. The Central Committee for the Great Jubilee held its first international meeting on February 15–16, 1996. Among the eight commissions under the Central Committee is a historico-theological commission. The historical section of this commission resolved to concentrate on two questions, anti-Semitism and the Inquisition, leaving other questions for later study. From October 30 to November 1, 1997, this section held an international symposium in Rome with the goal of studying the facts and presenting them to the pope for his judgment.

Quite independently of the preparations for the Great Jubilee, the Gregorian University, on September 22–25, 1997, hosted an international symposium, "Good and Evil After Auschwitz." Cardinal Cassidy opened the conference with a "Word of Welcome." A number of distinguished Jewish theologians, including Emil Fackenheim, were among the speakers. These two symposia form part of the larger context in which the document *We Remember* should be read and understood.

INTENT OF THE DOCUMENT

As distinct from the statements of particular national hierarchies, *We Remember* is written from the perspective of the universal church. It does not attempt to single out the merits or failures of particular national groups, many of which have been treated in the statements previously noted.

According to Cardinal Cassidy, a major objective was to promote "among the Catholics in those countries that were far removed by geography and history from the scene of the *Shoah* an awareness of past injustices by Christians to the Jewish people and encourage their participation in the present efforts of the Holy See to promote throughout the Church 'a new spirit in Catholic-Jewish relations.'"[20] Addressing Catholics all over the world, the authors chose to speak with moderation and restraint so as not to alienate the readership envisaged.

While seeking to make its readers aware of the inadequacies of the Catholic response to the challenge of Nazi racism, the document had to be composed in a way that would not play into the hands of anti-Catholic propagandists who seek to establish that Christian faith itself is a source of anti-Semitism and that the Catholic Church is by its very nature hostile to Judaism. This twofold objective accounts for a certain ambivalence that some have sensed in the document. While some sections sound a penitential note, others are more defensive in tone.

This commentary will not undertake a full analysis of the document, which is for the most part self-explanatory. It will simply address a few points that have occasioned criticism or puzzlement.

THE CHURCH AND ITS MEMBERS

Some readers have had problems with the distinction between the "Church as such" (which is regarded as holy and undefiled) and the "members" or "sons and daughters" of the church (who are acknowledged to be prone to sin). This distinction appears in an address by John Paul II to the

Gregorian University symposium, "The Roots of Anti-Semitism," in a passage quoted in section III of *We Remember.* The same distinction underlies the quotation from the apostolic letter *Tertio Millennio Adveniente* in section I.

The distinction between the church itself and the members of the church has a long and venerable history. Cardinal Giacomo Biffi, an authority on the question, traces it back at least to the fourth-century father, St. Ambrose, who wrote that the sins of Catholics wound the church "not in herself but in us."[21] The same distinction was used by Pius XII in his encyclical on the church (*Mystici Corporis,* 1943) and is implied in a number of texts of Vatican II which declared that the church contains sinners but avoided speaking of the church herself as sinful. Before and after the council the distinction was championed by prominent theologians such as Cardinal Charles Journet.[22]

These authors explain that for a theological understanding of the church one must see it from above, as coming from God through the action of Christ and the Holy Spirit. Theologically speaking, the church is the body and bride of Christ and the temple of the Holy Spirit. The members of the church would be sinless if they were totally molded by the church itself, but in fact they are molded only in part by the church. Their conduct reflects their own sinfulness and the influence of the world in which they live. When they act according to the principles of the church, guided by the Holy Spirit, the Word of God, and the sacraments, they avoid religious error and are free from sin. But apart from the Blessed Virgin and possibly a few other very eminent saints, the members of the church sometimes go astray. When they sin, they do so not because of but in spite of the fact that they are Catholics. To that extent they impair their union with the church. Their sins, as Cardinal Biffi expresses it, are "ontologically extra-ecclesial," since they do not come from the church and since they alienate the members in some degree from the church itself.

When the pope and the document *We Remember* speak of the "members" or "children" of the church, they are not referring to the laity alone. These terms apply to all members, including popes, cardinals, bishops, priests, religious, and laity. All of them can sin and err, but when they do so their action cannot be imputed to the church itself.

This theological distinction has obvious implications for our present theme. The church as such inculcates great love and respect for the Jewish people. But members of the church, because they may misunderstand the implications of their sacred heritage, can profess erroneous views and harbor un-Christian sentiments. Since Vatican II serious efforts have been made to revise Catholic catechetical materials to prevent deviations of this kind.

ANTI-JUDAISM AND ANTI-SEMITISM

A second issue that requires some discussion is the distinction made in section IV between anti-Judaism and anti-Semitism. Anti-Judaism is a theological attitude that has regrettably existed among Christians at various times and places. Prior to Vatican II it was often taught at the popular level that the Jews were collectively responsible for the death of Christ. This belief, supported by misunderstandings of some New Testament passages, fueled hostility toward the Jews, even though such hostility was contrary to the love and forgiveness taught by Christ and the saints. Christ and the early martyrs prayed for God's mercy on all who were in any way responsible for their death (Luke 23:34; Acts 7:60). The anti-Jewish interpretations of the New Testament, as the document recalls in section III, "have been totally and definitively rejected by the Second Vatican Council."

Anti-Semitism, as the document defines it, is a form of hostility based on nationalist and racist grounds. The anti-Semitism of the Nazis was a thoroughly neo-pagan phenomenon. Hitler taught that the Jews were corrupt by reason of their race. They could in no way be redeemed, even if they renounced their religious and ethnic heritage. According to this ideology all Jews, because they lack pure Aryan blood, must be shunned, even eliminated.

This racist ideology was totally opposed to Christian theological principles and, as *We Remember* points out, logically led to a rejection of Christianity, which teaches the dignity of every human person, the doctrine of universal love, and the unique role of the Jews in God's salvific plan. Anti-Semitism, unlike anti-Judaism, had a nontheological origin. In its National Socialist form it derived from idolatrous nationalism and a false biology of race.

We Remember does not deny that anti-Judaism, where it was allowed to germinate, may have made some Christians less sensitive and even indifferent to the persecutions launched by the Nazis. The document implies that further study is needed to explore the connections. But at the same time it observes that anti-Semitism in Europe, even before the rise of Hitler, was "more sociological and political than religious."

The problem, indeed, has multiple dimensions. "Historians, sociologists, political philosophers, psychologists and theologians are all trying to learn more about the *Shoah* and its causes" (section II). In a longer document it would have been necessary to analyze the sociological and psychological dimensions more extensively. All human societies, it would seem, are vulnerable to xenophobia and antipathy toward conspicuous minority groups in their midst. They tend to project their hostilities upon such groups, turning them into scapegoats. Antedating the rise of Christianity, anti-Semitism of a sort existed in Persia, Egypt, and throughout the Hellenistic empire. This attitude is enshrined in pagan authors such as Democritus, Cicero, Seneca, Apion, and Tacitus. The tensions between Christians and Jews cannot be fully understood without some familiarity with the dynamics of social psychology as well as particular historical memories.

To some degree Christian antipathy toward Jews is explicable in terms of Christian recollections of persecutions by Jews in the first century, which have left a deep trauma on the Christian imagination, just as the ghettos, pogroms, and forced conversions of the Middle Ages have continued to shape Jewish sensitivities. These frictions are humanly understandable, but they must not be used to justify the hatred and vengefulness sometimes displayed on the one side or the other.

It would be a fatal error for either Jews or Christians to dwell on the injustices of the past in such a way as to rekindle ancient animosities. What is needed, as John Paul II has said in various contexts, is a "healing of memories." The present document speaks of the need for a "moral and religious memory" that comes to terms with the past and overcomes its limitations (section II). To purify our hearts from resentment we must repent the wrongs of which our own coreligionists have been guilty; we must ask forgiveness and extend forgiveness, resolving to build a future marked by mutual respect and love.

CATHOLIC RESPONSE DURING THE *SHOAH*

A third point that will continue to arouse reflection is the assessment of the conduct of Catholics during the years of the *Shoah*. Without going into the particularities of different countries, *We Remember* discusses, in one paragraph, the reactions of the church in Germany. It recalls the condemnation of Nazi ideology by a number of courageous bishops and priests whose names deserve to be rescued from oblivion.[23] While acknowledging that some Christians failed to give every possible assistance to the victims of persecution, the document fails to mention others who actively collaborated with the persecutors. In this respect *We Remember* falls short of those documents that have come from national groups of bishops, notably the German and the French.

Something must here be said about the conduct of Pope Pius XII, which has become a subject of acrimonious dispute. The document mentions this pope in a single sentence in section IV, noting what he "did personally or through his representatives to save hundreds of thousands of Jewish lives." In a lengthy footnote it calls attention to expressions of gratitude that came after the war from Jewish groups and individual Jews. Golda Meir, for example, wrote on the occasion of the death of this great pope: "When fearful martyrdom came to our people, the voice of the pope was raised for its victims. The life of our times was enriched by a voice speaking out about great moral truths above the tumult of daily conflict. We mourn a great servant of peace."[24]

The literature on Pius XII and the Jews is vast. Eleven volumes published by the Holy See reproduce the relevant archival materials.[25] Informative books have been written by Pinchas E. Lapide, Michael O'Carroll, Margherita Marchione, Ronald J. Rychlak, and others. The scurrilous charges occasioned by the play *The Deputy,* written by Rolf Hochhuth in 1963, have been refuted in innumerable articles, but the campaign of defamation still goes on.

The record makes it clear that Pius XII took great risks to protect and save as many Jews as he could. He personally sheltered thousands in the Vatican City and in his summer residence at Castel Gandolfo. He released monasteries and convents from the rule of cloister in order to make them available as hiding places. He used the Vatican's diplomatic immunity to shelter Jewish refugees until the arrival of British and American troops. Again and again he instructed the bishops of the various European nations to assist the Jews in every possible way. Under his direct orders papal representatives intervened in Spain, France, Belgium, Holland, Slovakia, Hungary, Romania, Bulgaria, Greece, and Turkey to stem the deportation of innocent victims to death camps.

Pius XII was far from silent. In two encyclicals (*Summi Pontificatus,* 1939, and *Mystici Corporis,* 1943), in his annual Christmas messages (especially that of 1942), and again in an address to the cardinals of June 2, 1943, he spoke out in terms that everyone recognized as repudiations of Nazi racist ideology. He would have wished to speak even more explicitly, but he listened to the pleas of many bishops in occupied countries to the effect that strident protests would provoke the persecutors to adopt yet harsher measures and imperil the church's capacity to shield Jews and facilitate their escape. The fierce reaction of Nazi officials to the efforts of the Dutch bishops to intercede on behalf of the Jews in 1942 and 1943 provided a grisly example.[26]

We can only conjecture what effect a ringing denunciation on the part of the pope would have had. Presumably it would have given the Axis powers an excuse for treating the church as an enemy power. They would have invaded the Vatican and searched Catholic churches, monasteries, and convents everywhere for Jewish refugees, including even Christians having Jewish blood. There is no proof that such action by the pope would have been of any help to the Jews. In the absence of clear evidence to the contrary we may respect Pius XII's assessment: "No doubt a protest would have gained the praise and respect of the civilized world, but it would have submitted the poor Jews to an even worse persecution."[27] The United States Deputy Chief of Counsel at the Nürnberg War Crimes Trials reached the same judgment: "Every propaganda move of the Catholic Church against Hitler's Reich would have been not only 'provoking suicide,' as [Alfred] Rosenberg actually stated, but would have hastened the execution of still more Jews and priests."[28]

It is true that the Vatican archives for the period have not yet been opened. To open the archives at this point, when some of the persons involved are still living, would be a violation of fixed Vatican policy and would actually settle nothing. We have the word of those who have researched the archives that they contain no information that would change the picture given by the published materials. The opening of the archives would not satisfy all critics, because they could still claim that the archivists had concealed or destroyed incriminating records. The ample body of available evidence is sufficient to dispel the cloud of suspicion surrounding Pius XII, which seems to rest on prejudice or fantasy.[29]

THE NEED TO REPENT

Finally, something must be said about the question of repentance. *We Remember* in section IV declares: "We deeply regret the errors and failures of those sons and daughters of the Church" who failed to protest against the treatment of Jews by the Nazis. In section V the document states that the Catholic Church "desires to express her deep sorrow for the failures of her sons and daughters in every age. This is an act of repentance (*teshuva*), since, as members of the Church, we are linked to the sins as well as the merits of all her children." Asked by a journalist whether the church was apologizing, Cardinal Cassidy replied: "This is an act of repentance, it's more than an apology."[30] The distinction between the two kinds of act is important. Apology is directed to people who have been harmed; it expresses a wish that one had done otherwise in the past. Repentance, however, is directed to God and includes a resolution of amendment for the future.

Most of us are reluctant to repent, even for our own misdeeds. When reminded of something like the *Shoah,* we tend to say: "I didn't do it; I wasn't even around when it happened. So why am I being asked to repent? Why not let bygones be bygones and get on with the future?"

At this point we have to face the very difficult question of solidarity in sin. The concept of collective guilt is a dangerous one. It is precisely that concept which convinced some Christians in the past that the Jews of today should be punished for what their forebears had done to Jesus and to the early church. To resurrect the concept of collective guilt by making all Catholics responsible for the complicity of relatively few in the *Shoah* would be reckless and unjust.

Demands for a formal apology, indeed, tend to resurrect the discredited principle of corporate guilt.

We Remember indicates a path through this maze of difficulties. In section V it refers to the unique nature of the church as a mystical communion in which all the members are benefited or harmed by one another's good or bad conduct. The Catholic doctrine of the communion of saints goes back to the teaching of St. Paul on the church as body of Christ. When individual Christians sin, the sanctity of the whole body is tarnished. By repentance for the sins of our fellow believers we can help to purify the church. Our penitence does not mean that we are personally guilty or that we should be punished for the sins of others, but that we lovingly take upon ourselves the task of repenting their misconduct in order to restore right order. If we do not sincerely regret the infidelities of our brothers and sisters in the faith, we could well be guilty of sharing in the attitudes at the root of their misconduct. Repentance will enable us to break with the sinful patterns of the past and to usher in a new and better future. It may evoke a response of forgiveness on the part of those who have been injured, so that the dark pages of history may cease to spawn recrimination.

THE BROADER PICTURE

When the Catholic Church denounces anti-Semitism, it regularly recalls that every kind of racism is sinful. *We Remember* calls attention to this broader context. Because of the unique position of the Jewish people in salvation history the *Shoah* is in some respects unique. John Paul II speaks of the terrible fate of the Jewish people on that occasion as "a symbol of the aberration of which man is capable when he turns against God."[31] But we must not forget that persecution is in every case evil and that genocide against any group should be denounced. Lest our condemnation be selective, the document quite properly recalls that in our own century totalitarian dictatorships have taken a toll of many millions in addition to the Jews who suffered so unjustly under Hitler. Mention is made in section IV of the massacre of the Armenians during and after World War I, the countless victims in Ukraine in the 1930s, the mass extermination of Gypsies, the killing fields of Cambodia, and similar atrocities. Unless we consistently oppose all such acts of barbarism, we cannot hope to build a civilization of love and decency.

CONCLUSION

We Remember does not purport to be a definitive statement. It acknowledges that much research remains to be done regarding the *Shoah* and its causes. It was intended to encourage what had already been recognized as "a new spirit…in Jewish-Catholic relations, a spirit which emphasizes cooperation, mutual understanding and reconciliation, good will and common goals, to replace the past spirit of suspicion, resentment, and distrust."[32] Pope John Paul II, in introducing *We Remember,* expressed his fervent hope that it might "help to heal the wounds of past misunderstandings and injustices. May it enable memory to play its necessary part in the process of shaping a future in which the unspeakable iniquity of the *Shoah* will never again be possible."

Since March 1998, further progress has been made in overcoming past disagreements about the *Shoah*. In November 1999 a new Jewish-Catholic panel was established to conduct a joint review of the papal archives during the Second World War. The International Theological Commission published in March 2000 "Memory and Reconciliation," a theological reflection on the penitential aspects of the Great Jubilee, which builds on *We Remember*. Pope John Paul II, in his prayer service at St. Peter's Basilica on March 12, 2000, devoted a special section to "Confession of Sins against Israel," in which he prayed that Christians would "acknowledge the sins committed by not a few of their number against the people of the covenant and the blessings, and in this way purify their hearts." This prayer, however, made no special mention of the *Shoah*.

During his visit to Jerusalem on March 23, 2000, the pope placed a copy of his March 12 request for pardon in a crack between the stones of the Western Wall. On the same day he gave stirring address at Jerusalem's Yad Vashem Holocaust memorial, in which he expressed the deep sadness of the Catholic Church at all acts of hatred and persecution directed against Jews by Christians at any time and place. He spoke of the need for silence at the memorial "because there are no words strong enough to deplore the terrible tragedy of the *Shoah*." He prayed that the sorrow of Christians for such tragedies would lead to a new future in which Jews and Christians would respect each other as fellow-adorers of the one Creator and spiritual descendants of Abraham.

On September 10, 2000, a group of 170 Jewish scholars in North America stated in a full-page advertisement in the *New York Times* that there has been an unprecedented shift for the better in Jewish-Christian relations. With reference to the Holocaust, the statement noted that too many Christians participated in, or were sympathetic to, Nazi atrocities against the Jews. Then it added:

But Nazism itself was not an inevitable outcome of Christianity. If the Nazi extermination of the Jews had been fully successful, it would have turned its murderous rage more directly to Christians. We recognize with gratitude those Christians who risked or sacrificed their lives to save Jews during the Nazi regime. With that in mind, we encourage the continuation of recent efforts in Christian theology to repudiate unequivocally contempt of Judaism and the Jewish people. We applaud those Christians who reject this teaching of contempt, and we do not blame them for the sins committed by their ancestors.[33]

These dramatic developments since the publication of *We Remember* indicate that that statement is achieving its purpose as a stepping-stone on the road to reconciliation. I trust that the present commentary may play some part, however small, in achieving greater solidarity between our respective faith-communities.

NOTES

1. Vatican II, *Nostra Aetate*, in *The Documents of Vatican II*, ed. Walter M. Abbott, S.J. (New York: America Press, 1966), no. 4.

2. *Guidelines on Religious Relations with the Jews*, in *Doing the Truth in Charity*, ed. Thomas F. Stransky and John B. Sheerin, 342–47 (New York: Paulist Press, 1982), 342.

3. Text in *Origins* 15 (July 4, 1985): 102–7.

4. The term *Shoah* (literally "catastrophe") is often taken as the equivalent of Holocaust, but the two terms, while referring to the same event, are quite different in origin and meaning. One author notes: "The name *Shoah* is better, because 'holocaust' connotes sacrifice rising to heaven, whereas *Shoah* rather connotes descent into the pit of dereliction" (Donald Nicholl, "Other Religions *(Nostra Aetate)*," in *Modern Catholicism: Vatican II and After*, ed. Adrian Hastings, 126–34 (New York: Oxford University Press, 1991), 133 n.1.

5. German bishops, "Auschwitz Commemoration," *Origins* 24 (February 16, 1995): 586; also in National Conference of Catholic Bishops (NCCB), *Catholics Remember the Holocaust* (Washington, D.C.: United States Catholic Conference, 1998), 10–11. The quotation is from the resolution "Our Hope" of November 22, 1975. The German bishops might also have quoted from their own pastoral letter of August 23, 1945, which stated: "Many Germans, also from amongst us,…have remained indifferent…at the time of the crimes; many through their attitude supported the crimes, many themselves have become criminals. Serious responsibility falls upon those who because of their position were able to know what was happening among us and who, through their influence, could have prevented such crimes and did not do so, indeed have rendered possible these crimes and in this way showed themselves in solidarity with the criminals" (quoted by Reinhard Neudecker, "The Catholic Church and the Jewish People," in *Vatican II: Assessment and Perspectives Twenty-Five Years After (1962–1987)*, ed. René Latourelle, 3:282–323 (New York: Paulist Press, 1989), 320 n. 61.

6. Poland's bishops, "Auschwitz Commemoration," *Origins* 24 (February 16, 1995): 588; in NCCB, *Catholics Remember the Holocaust*, 14.

7. Oscar Lipscomb, "Commemorating the Liberation of Auschwitz," *Origins* 24 (February 9, 1995): 561–64; in NCCB, *Catholics Remember the Holocaust,* 16–24.

8. Swiss Bishops' Conference, "Confronting the Debate About the Role of Switzerland During the Second World War," in NCCB, *Catholics Remember the Holocaust,* 26.

9. Church in France, "World War II and the Jews," *Origins* 27 (October 16, 1997): 304–5; in NCCB, *Catholics Remember the Holocaust,* 35–36.

10. John Paul II, *Crossing the Threshold of Hope* (New York: Alfred A. Knopf, 1994), 97–98; also Tad Szulc, *Pope John Paul II: The Biography* (New York: Scribner, 1995), 69.

11. Darcy O'Brien, *The Hidden Pope: The Untold Story of a Lifelong Friendship That Is Changing the Relationship Between Catholics and Jews* (New York: Daybreak Books, 1998).

12. John Paul II, "Homily at Auschwitz II," *Origins* 9 (June 21, 1979): 73.

13. George H. Williams, *The Mind of John Paul II* (New York: Seabury, 1981), 328.

14. John Paul II, "Address in Rome's Chief Synagogue," *Origins* 15 (April 24, 1986): 731.

15. This address is quoted in *We Remember,* section IV; cf. ibid., n. 19.

16. John Paul II, remarks at St. Peter's Square, April 18, 1993; *L'Osservatore Romano* (English ed.), April 21, 1993, 12.

17. John Paul II, "Letter to Archbishop May," *Origins* 17 (September 3, 1987): 183.

18. Quoted in Luigi Accattoli, *When a Pope Asks Forgiveness* (Staten Island, N.Y.: Alba House, 1998), 119.

19. John Paul II, Apostolic Letter *Tertio Millennio Adveniente,* November 10, 1994, §33.

20. Edward I. Cassidy, "Reflections: The Vatican Statement on the *Shoah,*" address to the American Jewish Committee, Washington, D.C., May 15, 1998; *Origins* 28 (May 28, 1988): 29.

21. "Non in se sed in nobis Ecclesia vulneratur," Ambrose, *De Virginitate,* 48, discussed in Giacomo Biffi, *Christus Hodie* (Bologna:

Edizioni Dehoniane, 1995), 23–24. Cf. Accattoli, *When a Pope Asks Forgiveness,* 63–64.

22. Charles Journet, *L'Église du Verbe Incarné* II, 2 (Bruges: Desclée De Brouwer, 1962), 1115–28; idem, "Le caractère théandrique de l'Église: source de tension permanente," in *L'Église de Vatican II* Unam Sanctam 51b (Paris: Éd. du Cerf, 1967), 299–311.

23. In particular, *We Remember* mentions the actions of Cardinal Adolf Bertram of Breslau, Cardinal Michael Faulhaber of Munich-Freising, and Blessed Bernhard Lichtenberg, provost of the Berlin cathedral.

24. Note 16 in *We Remember* mentions three Jewish representatives, Dr. Joseph Nathan, Dr. A. Leo Kubowitzki, and Golda Meir. The list could have been much longer. Pinchas E. Lapide, after citing many Jewish testimonies, adds his own comment: "No pope in history has ever been thanked more heartily by Jews for having saved or helped their brethren in distress" (*Three Popes and the Jews* [New York: Hawthorn, 1967], 229). Lapide estimates that "the Catholic Church, under the pontificate of Pius XII, was instrumental in saving at least 700,000, but probably as many as 860,000, Jews from certain death at Nazi hands" (ibid., 214).

25. *Actes et Documents du Saint Siège relatifs à la Seconde Guerre Mondiale* (Vatican City: Libreria Editrice Vaticana, 1965–81). The number of volumes is reckoned as either eleven or twelve, depending on how one counts volume 3, printed in two parts. The first volume was translated into English under the title *The Holy See and the War in Europe, March 1939–August 1940* (Washington, D.C.: Corpus Books, 1968). Volume 10, which deals with the period from January 1944 to July 1945, is summarized by one of its editors, Robert A. Graham, S.J., in his booklet *Pius XII's Defense of Jews and Others: 1944–45* (Milwaukee, Wis.: Catholic League for Religious and Civil Rights, 1987). Graham's essay is reprinted in *Pius XII and the Holocaust: A Reader* (Milwaukee, Wis.: Catholic League for Religious and Civil Rights, 1988). The essential content of the documentation is synthesized in one volume by Pierre Blet, S.J., *Pie XII et la Seconde Guerre Mondiale d'après les archives du Vatican* (Paris: Perrin, 1997); English translation, *Pius XII and the Second World War according to the Archives of the Vatican* (New York/Mahwah, N.J.: Paulist Press, 1999).

26. The Dutch bishops, while confessing that errors had been made, recalled in their 1995 statement on the *Shoah* "the courageous actions of the episcopacy then led by Archbishop J. de Jong"; text in NCCB, *Catholics Remember the Holocaust*, 22. The reference is to Johannes de Jong of Utrecht, who was raised to the cardinalate in 1946.

27. Quoted by Joseph L. Lichten in his Introduction to Graham, *Pius XII's Defense of Jews and Others*, 2–3. See also Lapide, *Three Popes*, 247.

28. Robert M. W. Kempner in a Letter to *Commentary*, quoted in Graham, *Pius XII's Defense of the Jews*, 36; also in Blet, *Pie XII*, 322.

29. Blet's conclusion (*Pie XII*, 326) is worth quoting: "The Pacelli pope declared that he was conscious of having done all that he could to prevent the war, to assuage its sufferings, and diminish the number of its victims. To the degree that documents permit one to penetrate human intentions, they point to the same conclusion. In the actual order, to assert that he himself, or someone else in his place, could have done more is to leave the field of history and venture into the thickets of fantasy and dream." For a different translation, see Blet, *Pius XII*, 289. See also Pierre Blet, S.J., "La leggenda alla prova degli archivi: Le riccorente accuse contro Pio XII," *Civiltà cattolica* 149:1 (March 21, 1998), 531–41.

30. Cardinal Cassidy as quoted in press release, Vatican City, March 17, 1988 (VIS); cf. *New York Times*, March 17, 1998, A1.

31. John Paul II, *Centesimus Annus*, no. 17.

32. Final Statement of the Prague meeting of the International Catholic-Jewish Liaison Committee, 1990; *Origins* 20 (September 20, 1990): 235.

33. One Hundred Seventy Scholars, "Jewish Statement on Christians and Christianity," *Origins* 30 (September 21, 2000): 225–28, at 227.

Address by
Edward Idris Cardinal Cassidy

I am pleased to have this opportunity of reflecting with you this morning on the document published by the Holy See's Commission for Religious Relations With the Jews on March 16 of this year titled "We Remember: A Reflection on the *Shoah*."

Our document is the result of a process of reflection that began with the visit of Pope John Paul II to the United States in September 1987, in the course of which there was an encounter with Jewish leaders. The suggestion was then made that the Vatican might produce a document on the relation of the church to the *Shoah*. This was taken up during a meeting in Rome in the summer of 1987 of representatives of the Holy See's Commission for Religious Relations With the Jews and of the International Jewish Committee on Interreligious Consultations, and my predecessor in the office of president of the Commission for Religious Relations With the Jews agreed that the commission would begin a study on this question. On the following day, Sept. 1, 1987, the participants in this meeting were received at Castel Gandolfo by Pope John Paul II, who affirmed the importance of the proposed document for the church and for the world.

In the years following that decision, the Holy See's Commission for Religious Relations With the Jews engaged in a process of consciousness raising and of reflection on the *Shoah* at several levels in the Catholic Church and in different local churches.

Work began on the document soon after I took over responsibility for the Holy See's commission in January 1990, and we set out with the idea that one single document would cover all that the Catholic Church throughout the world might wish to state on this great tragedy of the 20th century.

As the work proceeded, it became clear, however, that the experience and involvement of the local churches throughout the world in relation to the *Shoah* were very different. What the church in Germany or Poland would want to say in this regard would not be identical, and even their statements would not be appropriate for the particular churches in other continents.

The bishops' conferences in Germany, Poland, the Netherlands, Switzerland, Hungary and France went ahead and each issued a statement that while dealing with the same general topic, referred in a special way to the particular experience of the peoples in their countries. Italy followed by presenting last March 16 a formal letter to the Italian Jewish community strongly condemning anti-Semitism and deeply regretting the past treatment of Jews in Italy. The way was thus open to the Holy See to speak to and on behalf of the universal church.

It is important to keep this fact in mind as one reads the Vatican's statement. We address our reflection to "our brothers and sisters of the Catholic Church throughout the world," and "we ask all Christians to join us in meditating on the catastrophe which befell the Jewish people." And we conclude with an invitation to "all men and women of good will to reflect deeply on the significance of the *Shoah*," stating that "the victims from their graves and the survivors through the vivid testimony of what they have suffered have become a loud voice calling the attention of all of humanity. To remember this terrible experience is to become fully conscious of the salutary warning it entails: The spoiled seeds of anti-Judaism and anti-Semitism must never again be allowed to take root in any human heart."

It is also important for an objective understanding of the document to keep in mind that our commission saw in this initiative the possibility of promoting among the Catholics in those countries that were far removed by geography and history from the scene of the *Shoah* an awareness of past injustices by Christians to the Jewish people and encourage their participation in the present efforts of the Holy See to promote throughout the church "a new spirit in Jewish-Catholic relations: a spirit which emphasizes cooperation, mutual understanding and reconciliation, good will and common goals, to replace the past spirit of suspicion, resentment and distrust."[1]

In the "Guidelines and Suggestions for Implementing the Conciliar Declaration *Nostra Aetate,* 4" published on Dec. 1, 1974, the Holy See's Commission for Religious Relations With the Jews recalled that "the step taken by the council finds its historical setting in circumstances deeply affected by the memory of the persecution and massacre of the Jews which took place in Europe just before and during the Second World War." Yet, as the guidelines point out, "the problem of Jewish-Christian relations concerns the church as such since it is when 'pondering her own mystery' that she encounters the mystery of Israel. Therefore, even in areas where no Jewish communities exist, this remains an important problem."

Such a document had by its very nature to attract the attention of and not alienate those to whom it was addressed. As I stated in my presentation of this document on March 16, it is to be seen as "another step on the path marked out by the Second Vatican Council in our relations with the Jewish people," and I expressed our fervent hope at that time "that it 'will help to heal the wound of past misunderstandings and injustices' (Pope John Paul II)."[2]

WHAT THE DOCUMENT STATES

As we approach the close of one Christian millennium and the birth of a third Christian millennium, the church has been called by Pope John Paul II, in his apostolic letter *Tertio Millennio Adveniente,* to "become more fully conscious of the sinfulness of her children, recalling those times in history when they departed from the spirit of Christ and his Gospel and, instead of offering to the world the witness of a life inspired by the values of faith, indulged in ways of thinking and acting which were truly forms of counterwitness and scandal."[3]

The document "We Remember: A Reflection on the *Shoah*" is to be read in this context. Indeed, it concerns one of the main areas in which Catholics should seriously take to heart the pope's summons. While no one can remain indifferent to the "unspeakable tragedy" of the attempt of the Nazi regime to exterminate the Jewish people for the sole reason that they were Jews, the church has a special obligation to reflect on this "horrible genocide," "by reason of her very close bonds of spiritual kinship with the Jewish people and her remembrance of the injustices of the past." Moreover, "the *Shoah* took place in Europe, that is, in countries of long-standing Christian civilization."

This, states the document, raises the question of the relation between the Nazi persecution and the attitudes down through the centuries of Christians toward Jews. In such a short document it was not possible to dwell at any length on the history of these relations, but the text admits clearly the prevalence over many centuries of anti-Judaism in the attitude of the church toward the Jewish people. It acknowledges the "erroneous and unjust interpretations of the New Testament regarding the Jewish people and their alleged culpability," a "generalized discrimination" in their regard "which ended at times in expulsions or attempts at forced conversions, attitudes of suspicion and mistrust," while "in times of crisis such as famine, war, pestilence or social tensions, the Jewish minority was sometimes taken as the scapegoat and became the victim of violence, looting, even massacres."

While lamenting this anti-Judaism, the document makes a distinction between this and the anti-Semitism of the 19th and 20th centuries based on racism and extreme forms of nationalism, theories contrary to the constant teaching of the church on the unity of the human race and on the equal dignity of all races and peoples. The anti-Semitism of the Nazis was the fruit of a thoroughly neopagan regime, with its roots outside of Christianity and, in pursuing its aims, it did not hesitate to oppose the church and persecute its members also. The Nazi regime intended "to exterminate the Jewish people...for the sole reason of their Jewish origin."

No attempt is made in the document to deny that "the Jewish people have suffered much at different times and in many places" while bearing their unique witness to the Holy One of Israel and to the Torah. "But the *Shoah* was certainly the worst suffering of all. The inhumanity with which the Jews were persecuted and massacred during this century is beyond the capacity of words to convey. *All this was done to them for the sole reason that they were Jews*" (my emphasis).

That does not mean of course that the Nazi persecution of the Jews was not made easier by the anti-Jewish prejudices imbedded in some Christian minds and hearts. This is clear in the document. What we state, however, is that before making accusations against people as a whole or individuals, one must know what precisely motivated them in a particular situation.

There were members of the church who did everything in their power to save Jewish lives, even to the point of placing their own lives in danger. Many did not. Some were afraid for themselves and those near to them; some took advantage of the situation; and still others were moved by envy. Let me quote the document on this central point:

"As Pope John Paul II has recognized, alongside such courageous men and women (those who did their best to help), the spiritual resistance and concrete action of other Christians were not that which might have been expected from Christ's followers. We cannot know how many Christians in countries occupied by or ruled by the Nazi powers or their allies were horrified at the disappearance of their Jewish neighbors and yet not strong enough to raise their voices in protest. For Christians, this heavy burden of conscience of their brothers and sisters during the Second World War must be a call to penitence. We deeply regret the errors and failures of those sons and daughters of the church....

"At the end of this millennium the Catholic Church desires to express her deep sorrow for the failures of her sons and daughters in every age. This is an act of repentance (*teshuva*), since, as members of the church, we are linked to the sins as well as to the merits of all her children."

While remembering the past, the Vatican document looks to a new future in relations between Jews and Christians, reminding members of the church of the Hebrew roots of their faith and that the Jews are their dearly beloved brothers, indeed in a certain sense their "elder brothers."[4]

"We Remember" closes with the prayer "that our sorrow for the tragedy which the Jewish people have suffered in our century will lead to a new relationship with the Jewish people. We wish to turn awareness of past sins into a firm resolve to build a new future in which there will be no more anti-Judaism among Christians or anti-Christian sentiment among Jews, but rather a shared mutual respect, as befits those who adore the one Creator and Lord and have a common father in faith, Abraham."

RELATION TO OTHER SIMILAR STATEMENTS

The document "We Remember: A Reflection on the *Shoah*" is not to be seen as the final word on all the questions raised in this reflection. While we do not foresee any other statement from the Vatican in the near future, I am sure that our document will result in renewed study and discussion. Indeed, this has been happening already with the publication of important articles by historians on Pope Pius XII and the Second World War. The document itself notes that "much scholarly study still remains to be done."

It is also important not to take the present document in isolation from those already issued by the episcopal conferences of several European countries or from the numerous statements made by Pope John Paul II in the course of his pontificate. There is no contradiction in these various texts. There is a variety in the tone and in the emphasis placed on certain aspects of the question, due as I have explained to the context in which they were issued and to the audience being addressed.

It is not possible this morning to dwell at any length on these other declarations, but I would like to look for a moment at the Drancy statement of the French bishops, issued on Oct. 2, 1997. This document received almost universal praise from Jewish circles.

The Drancy statement refers in particular to the period of the Vichy government following the defeat of France by the German forces in 1940. While passing no judgment on the consciences of the people of that era nor accepting guilt for what took place at that time, the French bishops acknowledge that "too many of the church's pastors committed an offense, by their silence, against the church herself and her mission" in the face of the many laws enacted by the government of that time.

The bishops find themselves "obliged to admit the role, indirect if not direct, in the process which led to the *Shoah* which was played by commonly held anti-Jewish prejudices, which Christians were guilty of maintaining." At the same time they state: "This is not to say that a direct cause-and-effect link can be drawn between these commonly held anti-

Jewish feelings and the *Shoah*, because the Nazi plan to annihilate the Jewish people has its sources elsewhere."

REACTION TO "WE REMEMBER"

The publication of the Vatican document received an enormous amount of publicity worldwide. Our commission has been flooded with reactions from both Jewish and Catholic sources. I would like now to share with you an overall vision of these responses.

From the part of the Catholic Church—and it was to the members of this church that the document was primarily addressed—the reactions have been very positive. This, as I have already indicated, is important, for the document was intended as one that would teach, arouse interest and cause reflection within the worldwide Catholic community.

Many of the early comments from the Jewish community were instead distinctly negative. Such comments ranged from "Vatican document dismays Jews" (Australian Jewish News); "It is too late, after 53 years, and it's not enough" (Chief Rabbi Yisreal Lau); "Document skirts the issue of church's long silences—Jewish reaction is cool" (New York Times); "An equivocal apology hurts more than its heals" (Los Angeles Times); to expressions of disappointment that this document was less forthright than those issued by various European bishops' conferences (Rabbi Leon Klenicki); that the apology contained therein was "less than unreserved" (Melbourne Age); and so on.

Other Jewish reactions were more positive. While not denying that they would have wished for a more definitive statement or endorsing all the historical judgments contained in the document, these comments saw also positive aspects of the Vatican's statement: "Mea culpa is a good start" (Rabbi Raymon Apple, senior rabbi of the Great Synagogue Sydney; "The Vatican's welcome first step" (Dr. Paul Bartrop of Bialik College, Melbourne); "Jews didn't get everything they wanted, but what they got was so significant and it doesn't prejudice other important steps. The old things that gave rise to anti-Semitism are no longer part of Catholic doctrine" (Michael Berenbaum, president of the Survivors of the *Shoah* Visual History Foundation);[5] "It is my sense that the document, if read in the context of history, represents both a true act of Christian repentance and an act of *teshuvah*" (David Gordis, president of Hebrew College in Brookline, Mass);[6] "This is a dramatic statement" (Rabbi Kopnick of Fort Wayne).

Rabbi Kopnick in his comments points out a fact that many overlooked, namely: "The Vatican didn't have to do anything." Indeed, Sir Owen Chadwick, a British authority on the Vatican in the Second World War, in an article published in The Tablet on March 28, 1998, expresses the conviction that it would have been better to say nothing:

"The Holocaust is the most brutal thing that ever happened. There are still people who suffer from it. There are still people living who remember fathers or brothers or sisters who died in some camp in eastern Europe though they were innocent of wrong. Nothing that anyone could ever say in the way of apology or sorrow or repentance can ever be adequate; anything that is said is bound to be resented. If you wish to avoid resentment (which is a good thing to avoid), say nothing."

I cannot agree with this and was comforted by the reception given to the document in an editorial in The Philadelphia Inquirer, which received our document with this comment:

"The document released Monday by the Vatican, 'We Remember: A Reflection on the *Shoah*,' is a remarkable, perplexing text, at once an acknowledgment, an apology and a repentance. The very title is a breakthrough. How crucial that the Roman Catholic Church would tell the world 'We remember the Holocaust': That puts an end to three generations of official silence."

Judith Banki, program director of the Marc Tanenbaum Center for Interreligious Understanding, in a letter to the New York Times, indicates another aspect of our document that has been generally overlooked. In my presentation to the press March 16, I pointed out that the Jewish delegation at the Sept. 1, 1987, meeting with Pope John Paul II in Castel Gandolfo, expressed the conviction that a Vatican document on the *Shoah* "will contribute significantly to combating attempts to revise and deny the reality of the Shoah and to trivialize its religious significance for Christians, Jews and humanity." Judith Banki rightly, I believe, states that the document "We Remember: A Reflection on the *Shoah*" "stands as a clear rebuttal to an entire industry of Holocaust denial and revision. To some 800 million Catholic faithful and to the world at large, the church has said 'it happened.' One cannot explain away as of no significance a document of the Catholic Church, inadequate or not in the opinion of the Jewish community, which expresses repentance for the actions or silence of its members in regard to a tragedy of 50 odd years ago. That tragedy must have happened."

QUESTIONS RAISED IN THE DOCUMENT

One of the criticisms of the document we are reflecting upon is that it asks several important questions, but does not give a satisfactory reply to them. I would like to say a few words about three of these questions.

The first is "the relations between the Nazi persecution of the Jews and the attitudes down through the centuries of Christians toward Jews." It seems to me that it is particularly on this point that most disappointment has been expressed by Jewish leaders.

There can be no denial of the fact that from the time of Emperor Constantine on, Jews were isolated and discriminated against in the Christian world. There were expulsions and forced conversions. Literature propagated stereotypes, preaching accused the Jews of every age of deicide; the ghetto which came into being in 1555 with a papal bull became in Nazi Germany the antechamber of the extermination.

It is also true that the Nazis made use of this sad history in their attacks on the Jewish people, adopting symbols and recalling events of the past to justify their deadly campaign. It is also true, I believe, that a part of the indifference shown toward the mass deportations and brutality which accompanied these forced movements of helpless and innocent people was a result of the age-old attitudes of Christian society and preaching toward those considered responsible for the death of Jesus.

But to make a jump from the anti-Judaism of the church to the anti-Semitism of the Nazis is to misread the nature of the Nazi persecution. To quote from the Vatican document: "The *Shoah* was the work of a thoroughly modern neopagan regime. Its anti-Semitism had its roots outside of Christianity and, in pursuing its aims, it did not hesitate to oppose the church and persecute her members also."

The church can justly be accused of not showing to the Jewish people down through the centuries that love which its founder, Jesus Christ, made the fundamental principle of his teaching. Rather, an anti-Jewish tradition stamped its mark in different ways on Christian doctrine and teaching. "To the extent that the pastors and those in authority in the church let such teaching of disdain develop so long and that they maintained among Christian communities an underlying basic religious culture which shaped and deformed peoples' attitudes, they bear a heavy responsibility.... This is not to say (however) that a direct cause-and-effect link can be drawn between these commonly held anti-Jewish feelings and the *Shoah,* because the Nazi plan to annihilate the Jewish people has its sources elsewhere" (Drancy statement). "At no time did the church authorities seek to exterminate the Jewish people!"

A second question that perhaps needs some explanation is a distinction that the Vatican document makes between *the church* and the *members of the church.* In our document we quote Pope John Paul II, who stated in an address to the October 1997 Vatican symposium on "The Christian Roots of Anti-Judaism":

"In the Christian world—I do not say on the part of the church as such—erroneous and unjust interpretations of the New Testament regarding the Jewish people and their alleged culpability have circulated for too long, engendering feelings of hostility toward this people."[7]

This distinction—the church and the members of the church—runs through the Vatican document and is not readily understood by those who are not members of the Catholic Church. Let me state first that when we make this distinction, the term *members of the church* does not refer to a particular category of church members, but can include according to the circumstances popes, cardinals, bishops, priests and laity.

For Catholics, the church is not just the members that belong to it. It is looked upon as the bride of Christ, the heavenly Jerusalem, holy and sinless. We do not speak of the church as sinful, but of the members of the church as sinful—a distinction you may find hard to understand but one which is essential to our understanding of the church.[8] An editorial in the Philadelphia Inquirer on March 18, 1998, acknowledged that "in Catholic belief, it's impossible to conceive of the church, divinely ordained and inspired, itself falling into such evil error. But through free will, individual Catholics, even very prominent ones, could so sin."

And that brings me to the third question raised by the Vatican document, the responsibility of certain individual members of the church, holding the highest positions of responsibility. We have been criticized for mentioning by name some who spoke out against the Nazi ideology and anti-Semitism. The references to Pius XII, in particular, have been the object of much comment.

I think it important to give credit where credit is due. History will surely find guilty those who could have acted and did not, those who should have spoken and did not. We did not have the information that would have allowed us to enter into judgment of individuals who might have fallen within these categories.

As for Pope Pius XII, it is our conviction that in recent years his memory has been unjustly denigrated. You will all have read Kenneth Woodward's concise article "In Defense of Pius XII" in Newsweek of March 30. Why did we wish to bring Pius XII into our document? For the very reason that Kenneth Woodward wrote his article. Ever since the play of Rolf Hochhuth in 1963 *The Deputy,* monstrous calumnies regarding Pius XII and the period of the Second

World War have gradually become accepted facts, especially within the Jewish community. In one page, Woodward shows how unjust this process has been.

Already two important articles by historians have appeared supporting the claims made in the document "We Remember." One by Rev. Father Pierre Blet, SJ, published in La Civilta Cattolica on March 21 and reproduced in L'Osservatore Romano on March 27. Father Blet is one of those who has studied all the documents in the Vatican Archives for the period of the Second World War. The second is an article in German, *"Gerechtigkeit fur Papst Pius XII,"* by Professor Herbert Scambeck of the Johannes Kepler University of Linz, Austria, published recently in the Rheinischer Merrier.

LOOKING TO A COMMON FUTURE

"We Remember" calls on Catholics to renew the awareness of the Hebrew roots of their faith. It expresses deep sorrow for the failures of the sons and daughters of the church and states, "This is an act of repentance (*teshuvah*)." The church approaches with deep respect and great compassion the experience of extermination, the *Shoah,* suffered by the Jewish people during World War II and sees this as a binding commitment to ensure that "evil does not prevail over good as it did for millions of the children of Jewish people.... Humanity cannot permit all that to happen again." "Most especially," we read in the Vatican document, "we ask our Jewish friends 'whose terrible fate has become a symbol of the aberrations of which man is capable when he turns against God,' to hear us with open hearts."

Finally, we pray that our sorrow for the tragedy of the *Shoah* will lead to a new relationship between Catholics and Jews. Indeed we see this document as one step in the building up of that relationship.

I am well aware that declarations are not enough; the coming Christian jubilee calls for a real conversion, both internal and external, before God and before our neighbor. As members of the church, but also as ordinary members of the human race, past history questions us. The silences, prejudices, persecutions and compromises of past centuries weigh upon us. Is it possible for us, as human beings and as Christians, to kneel before God in the presence of the victims of all times to ask pardon and to hope for reconciliation? I believe that it is. And if it is possible, then we should do it without waiting or losing any time. Tomorrow may be too late. If we could heal the wounds that bedevil Christian-Jewish relations we would contribute to the healing of the wounds of the world, the *tiqqun 'olam* (the mending of the world), which the Talmud considers to be a necessary action in building a just world and preparing for the kingdom of the most high.

Our recent document appeals not only to Catholics, but to all men and women of good will to make this kind of reflection, and I would see a particular challenge there for those Christians—Catholics, Orthodox and Protestant—who seek to journey together along the ecumenical way of unity. Could they not join together in this act of *teshuvah*?

In his article published in The Jewish Advocate and already referred to above, David Gordis expressed the hope that Jews will see the document "We Remember" as a true act of Christian repentance and an act of *teshuvah*. He makes a comment that seems to me worthy of reflection when he writes:

"We have no *repentance* in Judaism: we have *teshuvah* or *return*. The difference is important. As Jews reflect on the past, we look to a positive reshaping of our behavior and our relationship with God and with our fellow human beings. It is inevitable that we have missed the mark in small ways and big ways. We are called on not to punish ourselves, but to reshape our lives, to refocus ourselves to the good and proper way, to the path of God."

And then he goes on to quote Pope John Paul II's letter accompanying the Vatican document on the *Shoah,* in which the fervent hope is expressed that this document will help heal the wound of the past and "enable memory to play its necessary part in the process of shaping a future in which the unspeakable iniquity of the *Shoah* will never again be possible." David Gordis himself then expresses the hope that the document will be read in this way and that Jews will "welcome it as another step in making the world a better place, safer and more secure for all people."

This, I believe, is the challenge that faces us, Jews and Christians, in the face of growing secularism, religious apathy and moral confusion, a place in which there is little room for God. We may feel secure in a pluralistic, liberal-orientated society, and there are good reasons to do so. Yet it might be wise to keep in mind the possibility that a society with little room for God may one day have little room for those who believe in God and wish to live according to his law and commandments.[9] Whenever we can give united witness to our common values we should do so.

In any case, I am convinced that Christians and Jews have today a new opportunity of contributing together to the well-being of the societies of which we are both members and indeed to the world in which we live. The possibilities are immense: the care and conservation of the environment; respect for life; the defense of the weak and oppressed; the place of women in society; the promotion of the family; the protection of children; opposition to all forms of racism and anti-Semitism (which can also take the form of anti-Zionism); the education of future generations; and so on.

On the theme of the family, the International Catholic-Jewish Liaison Committee, during its 1994 meeting in Jerusalem issued a joint statement on the importance of the family in society.[10] And the recent meeting of the committee which was held in Vatican City in March, issued a similar document on the environment.[11]

Besides the diverse possibilities of cooperation in the field of human rights, there are challenges for us to work together for the protection of the rights of religion, for dialogue with the other great religions of the world—with a special place in this context for dialogue with the believing followers of Islam, and for collaboration in the realm of culture.

This calls for "cooperation, *mutual* respect and understanding, good will and common goals," to quote once again the Prague 1990 statement of the International Catholic-Jewish Liaison Committee.[12] Jews and Christians must learn to listen to each other, to seek to understand the other as the other understands him/herself rather than approach the other with an attitude of criticism or wish to argue or enter into a debate, be open to and respect the other, work together without compromising their own faith or distinct identity, be seen as children of the one and only God who know that God loves them and wants all men and women to know and experience that love, to be together a "light to the nations."

With the document "We Remember: A Reflection on the *Shoah*," the Catholic Church has renewed its "binding commitment to ensure that evil does not prevail over good." We ask the Jewish community to take our hand and join us in this challenge.

Address to the
American Jewish Committee
May 15, 1998

NOTES

1. International Catholic-Jewish Liaison Committee, Final Statement, Prague 1990, Pontifical Council for Promoting Christian Unity Information Service, No. 75 (1990), p. 176.

2. Pope John Paul II, Letter to Cardinal Cassidy on "We Remember: A Reflection on the *Shoah*."

3. Ibid., *Tertio Millennio Adveniente*, 33.

4. Ibid., speech at the Rome synagogue, April 13, 1986, No. 4.

5. Quoted in an editorial, The Philadelphia Inquirer, March 18, 1998.

6. The Jewish Advocate, April 3–9, 1998.

7. L'Osservatore Romano, Nov. 1, 1996, p. 6.

8. Vatican Council II's *Lumen Gentium,* 8, distinguishes "the society furnished with hierarchical agencies and the mystical body of Christ" and states that they are not to be considered as two realities. "Rather they form one interlocked reality which is comprised of a divine and a human element." This reality is compared by the council to the mystery of the incarnate Word.

9. In the former East Germany, less than 25 percent of the population have a church affiliation. The area known as *Lutherland* (Sachsen-Anhalt, which includes names dear to Lutherans such as Wittenberg, Eisleben, etc.) was 90 percent Christian before the war. Only 7 percent today are Lutheran, 3 percent Catholic. There are a few Jews and Muslims. The rest are without a religion.

10. International Catholic-Jewish Liaison Committee, Final Statement, Jerusalem 1994.

11. Ibid., Final Statement, Vatican 1998.

12. PCPCU Information Service, No. 75 (1990), p. 176.

other volumes in this series

Stepping Stones to Further Jewish-Christian Relations: An Unabridged Collection of Christian Documents, compiled by Helga Croner (A Stimulus Book, 1977).

Helga Croner and Leon Klenicki, editors, *Issues in the Jewish-Christian Dialogue: Jewish Perspectives on Covenant, Mission and Witness* (A Stimulus Book, 1979).

Clemens Thoma, *A Christian Theology of Judaism* (A Stimulus Book, 1980).

Helga Croner, Leon Klenicki and Lawrence Boadt, C.S.P., editors, *Biblical Studies: Meeting Ground of Jews and Christians* (A Stimulus Book, 1980).

John T. Pawlikowski, O.S.M., *Christ in the Light of the Christian-Jewish Dialogue* (A Stimulus Book, 1982).

Leon Klenicki and Gabe Huck, editors, *Spirituality and Prayer: Jewish and Christian Understandings* (A Stimulus Book, 1983).

Edward Flannery, *The Anguish of the Jews* (A Stimulus Book, 1985).

More Stepping Stones to Jewish-Christian Relations: An Unabridged Collection of Christian Documents 1975–1983, compiled by Helga Croner (A Stimulus Book, 1985).

Clemens Thoma and Michael Wyschogrod, editors, *Understanding Scripture: Explorations of Jewish and Christian Traditions of Interpretation* (A Stimulus Book, 1987).

Bernard J. Lee, S.M., *The Galilean Jewishness of Jesus* (A Stimulus Book, 1988).

Clemens Thoma and Michael Wyschogrod, editors, *Parable and Story in Judaism and Christianity* (A Stimulus Book, 1989).

Eugene J. Fisher and Leon Klenicki, editors, *In Our Time: The Flowering of Jewish-Catholic Dialogue* (A Stimulus Book, 1990).

Leon Klenicki, editor, *Toward a Theological Encounter* (A Stimulus Book, 1991).

David Burrell and Yehezkel Landau, editors, *Voices from Jerusalem* (A Stimulus Book, 1991).

John Rousmaniere, *A Bridge to Dialogue: The Story of Jewish-Christian Relations;* edited by James A. Carpenter and Leon Klenicki (A Stimulus Book, 1991).

Michael E. Lodahl, *Shekhinah/Spirit* (A Stimulus Book, 1992).

George M. Smiga, *Pain and Polemic: Anti-Judaism in the Gospels* (A Stimulus Book, 1992).

Eugene J. Fisher, editor, *Interwoven Destinies: Jews and Christians Through the Ages* (A Stimulus Book, 1993).

Anthony Kenny, *Catholics, Jews and the State of Israel* (A Stimulus Book, 1993).

Eugene J. Fisher, editor, *Visions of the Other: Jewish and Christian Theologians Assess the Dialogue* (A Stimulus Book, 1995).

Leon Klenicki and Geoffrey Wigoder, editors, *A Dictionary of the Jewish-Christian Dialogue* (Expanded Edition), (A Stimulus Book, 1995).

Frank E. Eakin, Jr., *What Price Prejudice?: Christian Antisemitism in America* (A Stimulus Book, 1998).

Ekkehard Schuster & Reinhold Boschert-Kimmig, *Hope Against Hope: Johann Baptist Metz and Elie Wiesel Speak Out on the Holocaust* (A Stimulus Book, 1999).

Mary C. Boys, *Has God Only One Blessing?: Judaism as a Source of Christian Self-Understanding* (A Stimulus Book, 2000).

Peter Wortsman, editor, *Recommendation Whether to Confiscate, Destroy and Burn All Jewish Books* by Johannes Reuchlin (A Stimulus Book, 2000).

STIMULUS BOOKS are developed by Stimulus Foundation, a not-for-profit organization, and are published by Paulist Press. The Foundation wishes to further the publication of scholarly books on Jewish and Christian topics that are of importance to Judaism and Christianity.

Stimulus Foundation was established by an erstwhile refugee from Nazi Germany who intends to contribute with these publications to the improvement of communication between Jews and Christians.

Books for publication in this Series will be selected by a committee of the Foundation, and offers of manuscripts and works in progress should be addressed to:

Stimulus Foundation
c/o Paulist Press
997 Macarthur Boulevard
Mahwah, N.J. 07430
www.paulistpress.com